A Management Framework:
For project, program and portfolio integration

By R. Max Wideman, P.Eng.
FCSCE, FEIC, FICE, FPMI

This book is supported by extensive project management information on the companion website at www.maxwideman.com

Contact the author via www.maxwideman.com or Trafford Publishing

Note for Librarians: a cataloguing record for this book that includes Dewey Decimal Classification and US Library of Congress numbers is available from the Library and Archives of Canada. The complete cataloguing record can be obtained from their online database at: www.collectionscanada.ca/amicus/index-e.html

ISBN 1-4120-2786-1

Printed in Victoria, BC, Canada

Disclaimer

In general, the concepts expressed in this publication are in the public domain and may be used freely by individual readers in connection with their project work. They may not be appropriated by commercial or non-commercial organizations for their sole benefit. While the author and publisher have used their best efforts in preparing this work, neither assumes any responsibility for errors or omissions. Neither is any liability assumed for damages from the use of the information contained herein.

Production information

Desktop publishing in Adobe InDesign 3.0.1 for Apple Macintosh OS X 10.3.5. Diagrams in Canvas 9.0.3.

TRAFFORD

Offices in Canada, USA, Ireland, UK and Spain

This book was published on-demand in cooperation with Trafford Publishing. On-demand publishing is a unique process and service of making a book available for retail sale to the public taking advantage of on-demand manufacturing and Internet marketing. On-demand publishing includes promotions, retail sales, manufacturing, order fulfilment, accounting and collecting royalties on behalf of the author.

Book sales for North America and international:
Trafford Publishing, 6E–2333 Government St.,
Victoria, BC V8T 4P4 CANADA
phone 250 383 6864 (toll-free 1 888 232 4444)
fax 250 383 6804; email to orders@trafford.com

Book sales in Europe:
Trafford Publishing (UK) Ltd., Enterprise House, Wistaston Road Business Centre,
Wistaston Road, Crewe, Cheshire CW2 7RP UNITED KINGDOM
phone 01270 251 396 (local rate 0845 230 9601)
facsimile 01270 254 983; orders.uk@trafford.com

Order online at:
www.trafford.com/robots/04-0614.html

10 9 8 7 6 5 4 3 2

Foreword

It is among the most noble of human gifts – to share one's intellectual property – with no intended purpose other than knowing that others will benefit from that gift. Max Wideman's *A Management Framework: for project, program and portfolio integration*, is such a gift.

Max and I have dwelled in the halls of the project management community for over four decades. We started practicing project management when the discipline was still in diapers. It was not that long ago (April 1986), that a New York Times book review referred to project management as "arcane." That was not an inaccurate description. Even into the 80s, practitioners of project management were a rare breed and project management was yet to be recognized as a discipline in its own right.

Max clearly recognized this deficiency and has devoted his career to correcting it. In December 1984, as incoming president of the Project Management Institute ("PMI"), I wrote: "our challenge is to define the project management body of knowledge, to identify and improve areas of weakness, and to tie a ribbon around it." Max took that as a battle cry and unrelentingly dedicated the past three decades to promoting standards for project management.

In *A Management Framework for Project, Program and Portfolio Integration,* Max captures the essence of the standards and practices that have grown from a small kernel of theory in the late 50s to form the basis for modern project management. Today, these practices are enjoying universal application, across every describable industry. Today, project management is experiencing phenomenal growth, both in the numbers of trained practitioners and in the breadth of the discipline, itself.

While the body of knowledge rapidly expands, it is important that we capture and publish the fundamental practices that formed the foundation of modern project management. This book serves that purpose. Project Management is often called the "Accidental Profession." I can't argue with that. My own experience (a common one at that) was to find myself in a career change in 1962 – applying fundamental project management practices without ever having been trained in the craft. There was very little published material on project management. Most of what was available referred to very specific applications, based on the use of the first PERT and CPM software programs. But over the years, the craft has been well documented and there is no excuse for the "swim or sink" situation that I faced over four decades ago.

Using this swim or sink reference, many of us can recall having learned to swim by being thrown in the pond to fend for ourselves. Staying on top of the water is such a natural response that we soon find that we can swim. Such is often the case in project management. We get thrown into the pool and are expected to swim across, relying on our common sense to deal with the complex issues of project management. Many of us rise to the occasion and (somewhat clumsily) get the job done. Others panic and thrash around in the water while the project performance goes down the drain. It doesn't have to be that way.

There are several views of project management as a discipline. Some believe that project management is a compendium of practices and procedures, backed up by a bevy of intimidating and cryptic computer programs. At the other end of the spectrum is the belief that project management depends on personal leadership. All that is needed to achieve project success is a charismatic manager with some clout. Strangely, there is some truth to both of these widely separate views. An effective project management capability requires some of both of these styles.

Yet, there is so much more to the equation. There is the matter of organizational design, organizational culture and clearly visible sponsorship by senior executives. These are required to transform an organization from a day-to-day ongoing business mode to one that maximizes the contribution of projects to the firm's success. There is the infusion of skills and knowledge in new areas of work management and communication. There is the often-overlooked need to integrate the various components and disciplines of the firm so that everyone is on the same page. Although the language of each discipline is often unique to that group, the language gap must be bridged so that the knowledge and contributions of each can be funneled into the successful project operation.

So while each of us must continue to execute our individual functions, the project's environment demands that we acquire at least a basic understanding of this growing world of project management. If we want to make intelligent and useful contributions to the project process and to project success, we need to learn the details about our specific contribution area and gain at least an overview of the entire project management discipline, so as to better understand where our part fits.

This book supports all of this and more. The reader is offered a view of project management from almost every angle. For an overview, there is the perspective of project management from 30,000 feet. Where you find interest or need, you can swoop down for a closer look. The contents reflect the perspective and wisdom of someone who has practiced project management for as long as it has been recognized as a discipline of its own. Here, we have common sense, laid out in a readable style. You can take this stuff and run with it. You can commit it to memory and easily share it, understandably, with others.

A significant portion of the book is devoted to the project environment and culture. We are shown how to go about establishing a project management capability and why we should do what is prescribed. There is a plethora of books that present the nuts and bolts of project management in excruciating detail. Here we have a clear look at the environment in which we employ the nuts and bolts, in addition to a practical look at key details. Having this framework makes everything else more understandable. The discipline of project management can be considered to be both an Art and a Science. Both aspects receive comparable attention in the book.

It is obvious that the book has been brought up to date by the inclusion of a couple of very important chapters on Project Portfolio Management (PPM). The recognition and structuring of PPM during the past five years has raised the value of projects and project management to a new level. It has allowed us to bridge the gap between the projects side of the organization and the operations side of the business. PPM enables us to not only do projects right, but to do the right projects. There is much to learn from these two new chapters. If this whets your appetite for more on the subject of PPM, you are invited to review my own new book on the subject: *Project Portfolio Management: A Practical Guide to Selecting and Prioritizing Projects*, scheduled for publication by the Jossey-Bass div. of John Wiley & Sons, in July 2005.

If, in reading Max's book, you can generate just a small percentage of the enthusiasm and skills that Max and I have derived from our own long involvement in the field of project management, you will find that your work will become more productive and satisfying. Forgive me for using such an old cliché – May your reading of this book become a journey, rather than a destination. And may we meet up with you along the road and share in the joy of the trip.

Harvey A. Levine
PMI Fellow and past Chair

Harvey Levine is author of:

- *Project Management Using Microcomputers*, Osborne McGraw-Hill, 1986
- *Practical Project Management: Tips, Tactics, and Tools*, John Wiley & Sons, 2002
- *Project Portfolio Management: A Practical Guide to Selecting and Prioritizing Projects*, Jossey-Bass, 2005

The Project Knowledge Group
San Diego, CA and Saratoga Springs, NY
July 2004

Preface

Welcome to project management !

If you are new to project management, then welcome to this exciting world! I hope that this book *A Management Framework: for project, program and portfolio integration* will provide you with a head start. If you are an "old hand", then I hope that it will provide you with some new ideas and reference material to convince your colleagues of the importance of project management, what it means and why.

Professor Pinto once observed that:

> "Project management is a philosophy and technique that enables its practitioners to perform to their maximum potential within the constraints of limited resources, thereby increasing profitability . . . With the future bright for expanding the role of project management on a worldwide basis, the only potential clouds on the horizon concern the ability of governments and businesses to use these techniques well. The lack of formal training for many future project managers is worrisome and must be corrected. We must continue our efforts to develop a common skill set and body of knowledge so that these techniques can be used to their maximum potential."[1]

Your own interest may be in small administrative projects, management projects, large-scale capital works, or a whole program of projects. Perhaps managing a project is your chosen career or just a fleeting career obligation. And, whether the project itself is public, private or personal, I hope to provide you with some fascinating insights into the expectations, processes and satisfaction of managing projects successfully.

When I wrote the first version of this book in 1991, there were relatively few textbooks on project management. Today there are many so you might well ask, "yet another one?" However, I have had the opportunity to review many of these books and found that they vary considerably in clarity and usefulness. Mostly they promote either one particular author's way of doing things or simply regurgitate some organization's established mantra.

In this book I wish to do neither. True, it will be my view of the project management world, but what I hope to do is to bring together and introduce the reader to some basic insights resulting from my practical experience. Some of these things seem to me to be obvious and fundamental yet, in my opinion, still seem to be overlooked in the standard project management treatise. And that is a pity because I have found these things help me considerably in understanding what is going on.

Of course the need for managing projects is far from new. Records of major projects abound since early history and these projects have always been managed for better or worse, by design or default, according to the skill, intuition and luck that the manager could muster at the time. But today we live in an age of unprecedented change that must be actively and carefully managed for our very survival. Therefore, there has been a growing recognition that management, and particularly project management, requires special skills that must be codified and learned. These skills are essentially different from those associated with managing the main technology of the project such as construction, organizational change, software development, research and development, and so on.

Some people ask me, "Can the two disciplines of technology management and project management really be separated?" My answer is, philosophically yes, but practically, no! So be warned, this book is as much philosophical as it is practical. I will leave the management of any given technology to the experts in their respective fields.

This book's structure

This book is divided into five main sections:

Part I looks at the management of projects from the outside and from a number of different viewpoints. It provides the reader with the basis for further reading and study

Part II examines a number of common attributes found in all project work. It displays these as models or diagrams designed to provide a mental image of project management and its various aspects.

Part III explores the uniquely dynamic nature of project management, principally as it affects and is viewed by those working from the inside of the process. It deals with the practical realities of a project and so is possibly the most challenging and of most immediate use.

Part IV expands the horizon by taking a look at program and portfolio project management, how these can be managed, and what effect this has on the knowledge base. In this section we also take a more advanced look at portfolio project selection.

Part V provides our final thoughts with a focus on success and the future of project management.

For brevity and ease of reference, I have deliberately tried to present the subject matter in simple and concise terms, often in bullet format or by graphic illustrations. I hope you will find it informative, stimulating and helpful reading.

Acknowledgements

My early interests in documenting a Project Management Body of Knowledge, or PMBoK as it was originally referred to, started in the early 1980s. Friends and colleagues, including many in the Project Management Institute ("PMI"), have been very enthusiastic and supportive in identifying knowledge that is significant and perhaps unique to managing projects successfully. Over the years, many individuals have contributed from their experience to this venture, so that we have seen a steady improvement in our understanding of the project management discipline.

First came the development of an Ethics, Standards and Accreditation report by the late Matt Parry, published by the Project Management Institute around 1983. The objective of the report was to enable PMI to establish the necessary attributes for establishing a certification program, one of the building blocks for establishing a profession of project management. The standards then consisted of the project management subjects of scope, quality, time, cost, human resources and communications.

As Chairman of PMI's PMBOK Standards Board at the time, I recognized the importance of this work and sought to expand the base by adding risk management and contract/procurement management. With the help of many contributors, a formal publication of the "Project Management Body of Knowledge (PMBOK)" was approved and published by the Institute in 1987. For the record, "PMBoK" (small "o") is a term that I invented. Since then, the Institute has replaced this document with "A Guide to the Project Management Body of Knowledge", better known as "PMBOK® Guide", or just the "Guide". This, in turn, has been updated several times as a result of prodigious efforts by many people over extended periods.

The Guide as currently presented is certainly more readable and meaningful to many people than the 1987 edition, especially for those in the systems fields who are comfortable with systems inputs and outputs. However, it should be remembered that the Guide is a guide to the main elements of the project management body of knowledge and as such is a vehicle for education and certification purposes. It is not, nor is it intended to be, a methodology for running a project.

If what we now have is a "guide" to the PMBOK, then where do we go to find out what that PMBOK itself is? Some would argue that it is simply the collective works of all published material on the subject. Perhaps. But considering the differing opinions out there, to say nothing of outright contradictions, that is hardly satisfactory. There is probably no good answer to this question, but as a follow on to my original work on the PMBOK, I took advantage of Internet technology to establish a web site with comprehensive coverage of project management.

On this site I have published what I consider to be basic information about project management, or how to perform the project manager's many responsibilities. I believe that this information should all be in the public domain and available to anyone interested in the subject. In this book I hope to add to that knowledge and at the same time perhaps clarify or even correct some of the misunderstandings that I think some people still have.

To the many who have helped to shape my thinking, and hence contribute directly or indirectly to this book, or to the contents of my web site, I offer you all a most humble but hearty "thank you". The best ideas are theirs but the mistakes are obviously mine. I am particularly indebted to Russ Archibald, Paul Giammalvo, Harvey Levine, Lee Merkhofer, Rita Mulcahy, Penny Schneider and Barbara White, the reviewers of the drafts of this book who have pointed out errors and helped to make the book more readable.

You can find my web site at http://www.maxwideman.com.

R. Max Wideman
Fellow, PMI

References

[1] Pinto, J. K., Project Management: The Future, in Project Management for Business Professionals: A Comprehensive Guide, NY: Wiley, 2001, p586

Table of Contents

Part III: Project Dynamics

List of Figures

I have thought that a man of tolerable abilities may work great changes,
if he first forms a good plan and makes execution of that same plan
his whole study and business

Benjamin Franklin

Part I Project Management

CHAPTER 1

Introduction

1.1 Where should we start?

As an engineer and long-time project manager I've been trained to think that the right place to start is at the beginning: "What is a project?", "What is project management?", that sort of thing. And so it should be except for one remarkable fact. It seems to be a quirk of human nature, and this is especially true of people on projects, that the best starting point is not at the beginning but somewhere in the middle. People just like to jump in somewhere, anywhere, mosey around a bit, find out if they like what they see, and then make a decision.

The SCOPE-PAK© method is a good way to start the planning of a project

Whoever reads the first chapter to decide if they want to buy a book? The sequence is much more likely to be: front cover, back cover and then flip the pages *from back to front!*

Another good example is in project planning by the SCOPE-PAK© method.[1] This is a one-hour brain storming exercise in getting team buy-in for the development of a complete project plan. You might think you would start with the project's goals and objectives, but you would be wrong. First you should identify the stakeholders so that you know whom you are serving. Then goals and objectives? No. Everyone will have a vague idea, but each one of them different, so there is no point in trying to fine-tune a project scope definition at this stage and enduring an interminable argument!

Better by far is to "work the problem" and start people thinking about the things that have to be done.

Let people get those issues off their chests, so to speak, and that will free up their minds to make a real contribution to the question: "What are we really here to accomplish?" Now, finally, we've got to the goals and objectives. And so it is with this book. In this chapter we'll start with the people we serve as project managers, followed by some general observations about the project environment, then answer the question "Do we really need this book?"

1.2   Who is project management really for?[2]

A common thread runs through all of the following examples of real-life successful undertakings:[3]

A common thread runs through all these examples

- Planning, financing, designing, building, opening, operating or leasing institutional, commercial, industrial, or infrastructure facilities in most major population centers in recent years – your traditional construction project.

- The completion of a major revamp, upgrade and expansion to an oil refinery or other industrial process facility to meet a previously agreed schedule and budget without crippling the existing production operations – your typical industrial process project.

- Any of the multitude of NASA space program projects at the Johnson Space Center, examples of highly innovative high-technology projects.

- Open-heart surgery operating room practices now routine for the operating team, but unique to the patient. These require careful management planning to optimize the process.

- The development, production and distribution of a new software product, including the accompanying advertising and sales program. The nature of the work itself is challenging and the asset value of the product is in its intellectual application and not in its physical presence.

- The successful organization of conferences. The lead-time is long, the number of stakeholders is large but the product, the conference itself, is relatively brief. For many, the organization of conferences has become routine, but each conference is different by virtue of its time, place and subject matter, and success, by whatever measure, is high on the risk scale.

- Then there is the host of corporate business projects such as improvements in administrative procedures in order to remain competitive. These are not always seen as projects but they are nonetheless initiatives that can benefit considerably from the appropriate application of project management.

The list of possible projects is almost endless, but this should be a sufficient sample. The issue is: what is the common thread?

1.3   Common thread and who benefits

All of the examples cited above feature one common result: they are about change. And change brings about something new, whether that is a new artifact, a new way of doing things, or a new attitude. Such change can be done well or it can be done poorly, and the difference is in how the project is managed, or even if the project is managed at all.

All projects do need managing, yet many just limp along at a fraction of their potential simply because people don't know how to make them run any better. Since the result has a direct impact on the "bottom-line", we may conclude that project management:

- Is of value to every organization determined to manage their change efforts successfully.

A good leader knows the right thing to do, a good team knows how to do it right

- Is of value to all those who play a part in implementing corporate strategy, especially the transitions necessary to keep pace with the technological evolution of the modern world, and

- Runs the gamut from the people-in-the-trenches to the chief executive, to say nothing of all the other stakeholders involved.

For the project manager, it is worth noting that a good project leader knows the right things to do, a good team knows how to do things righdealt. To such a group project change is welcomed rather than feared, because the art of orientation and winning support is part and parcel of being an effective team player. To achieve these ideals, you must know what to expect and what to do.

So, all projects demand explicit management attention, whatever their nature, size or duration. However, the type of attention that they receive should depend on the special features of the individual project. For example:

- Rarity
- Constraints
- Complexity
- Dynamic response
- Multi-discipline

- Multi-stakeholders
- Uncertainty
- Technology and other factors

Each of these is explained in the next section.

1.4   Special features of projects

The special features of projects can be categorized as follows:

Rarity

Projects are unique or relatively infrequent undertaking for one reason or another by virtue of their end objectives and/or environment. It could be argued that building a house is not a project because people build houses all the time. Not so. Any given house is particular to a given owner, is on their land, at a particular time and with their money. In these respects, the project is different from any other project.

Constraints

Projects typically include internal objectives that become constraints in the hands of those responsible for actual execution. For example:

- A certain quality standard or quality grade in the finished product

- Limited time frame (i.e. the time available up to delivery of the product)

- Limited resources (e.g. the people, skills, equipment and materials available for the work)

- Limited money (i.e. a specified budget)

Complexity

Complexity can take several forms:

- The goals, objectives and constraints may not be compatible and will require resolution

- Opposing interests of stakeholders, real or fabricated, both internal and external, will require resolution

- The interaction of different technologies may create problems that will require resolution

- Technology improvements or upgrades may require incorporation
- The technology itself may be complex

Dynamic response

- The need for visibility of the project as an agent of change during its execution
- The need to be responsive to external changes during the life of the project
- The need to be responsive to internal developments reflected by the project life span

Multi-discipline

Even in a unified project team, there will inevitably be multiple contributors. Consequently:

- Their contributing efforts and interests will require integrating
- When more than one discipline is involved, these contributions will require coordinating, often across organizational boundaries
- Separate skills will require careful coordination

Multi-stakeholders

"Stakeholder" is the name we give to anyone who has a "stake" in the execution or outcome of the project. Because each stakeholder is likely to have a different perspective and personal vested interest, there are likely to be conflicts of interest. So:

- "Stake" is used here in the sense of creating a risk
- That risk may be positive if the stakeholder is generally in favor of the project but negative if they are not, or just "reluctant beneficiaries"
- This means that each stakeholder's "requirements", whether overt or covert, must be given some consideration
- There may also be interdependencies between stakeholders that must also be taken into account, adding to the project's complexity

Uncertainty

By virtue of its "uniqueness", the outcome of a project is uncertain. This could mean that there will be opportunities to increase the benefit from the project just as much as there will be risk events that could reduce it. The probability of less than optimum results, or even failure, must be set against the opportunity for positive gain.

Technology and other factors

Some other factors worthy of consideration:

- An appreciation of the effect of the project on the participating organizations and/or user environment is crucial
- A broad-based understanding of the technology is required
- The appropriate technical skills must be found or established for both project execution and product use
- Day-to-day project issues must be dealt with in a timely manner
- Competent project management expertise is essential for project managing the technology
- Substantial sponsor commitment to the technology is needed

1.5   The benefits of effective project management

Project management increasingly plays a central role in the management of successful companies

For many business administrations, project management has become a way of life instead of being geared only to large, unique special assignments. Consequently, the benefits of a sound project management approach are now receiving greater recognition than ever and project management is playing a much more central role in the mainstream management of successful companies. Why? Because changes in the global marketplace are commonplace, competition is more fierce and organizations face increasing pressures in an unforgiving arena.

The use of project management techniques in developing both products and services and the processes (i.e., marketing, procurement, manufacturing, quality and after-sales services, etc.) required to get those products or services to the customer on a more timely basis is increasingly critical to the success of the venture.[4] Senior managements increasingly recognize the advantages of flatter, more flexible team-based approaches in dealing with the really important issues, especially those that cut across the organization as a whole.[5]

1.6   The project management potential

Growth, change and projects go together. In an increasingly turbulent world, business becomes faster-paced, more complex and more competitive. So, the rewards go to those organizations that are:[6]

- More flexible
- More in tune with their customers' wants
- More focused on their main product or service
- More professional in every aspect of their business, and
- Heavily committed to continuous learning

Project management masters an ever-changing environment

For an organization, modern project management specifically sets out to deal with an ever-changing environment. With flexible project teams focused on the needs of the enterprise, project-based planning and implementation aligns corporate resources with corporate strategy and initiatives. For the individual, managing projects helps to develop qualities of initiative and effectiveness that senior management looks for in promoting staff for advancing its organization.

Some corporate cultures are much more supportive of project working than others. Consequently, top managers who plan to introduce the project management discipline into their organization, or who wish to improve existing project performance, must pay attention to the existing cultural, structural, practical and personal elements. This is because project management:

- Requires team-working skills, rather than a rigid bureaucratic structure

- Values quality information, discipline and goal-orientation rather than mindless adherence to antiquated procedures

- Has a primary focus on what has yet to be done, and who will do it, rather than on records of past achievements

- Has become as much about attitudes and motivation as it is about tools and techniques

Interestingly, the major project management organizations in the world share a strong perception that the creative concept of project management is universal and generic, crosses all cultural, national and linguistic barriers, and many of the problems inherent in creating change or adapting to change are common to all.[7]

1.7   What it takes to succeed

For project management to succeed and its benefits to be realized, three ingredients must first be in place, namely:[8]

- Support from senior authority
- Agreement and commitment at the level of responsibility, and
- A willing acceptance of the product at the level of impact

As Konosuke Matsushita, Executive Director of Matsushita-Electric observed when comparing Western and Japanese management styles:

> ". . . for us, the core of management is precisely the art of mobilizing and pulling together the intellectual resources of all employees . . . only by drawing on the combined brainpower of all its employees can a firm face up to the turbulence and constraints of today's environment."

A technical manager may or may not have the necessary project management skills

Project managers are often selected for their technical competence alone, perhaps because management has a better appreciation of the technological skills required, or perhaps because they feel that anyone can "do project management". However, the probability of this working out is low for two good reasons:

- A person competent in delivering work may or may not have the skills and inclination to manage, let alone have training in project management

- When they get the chance, most people like to revert to their comfort zones. Therefore, they are more comfortable doing the work than spending the time on instructing others how to do it.

A project manager needs to know enough about the technical nature of the work to be able to understand the issues that arise and avoid being duped by the "experts". However, the primary areas of competence required by any project manager include:

- Clear and unequivocal communication
- The ability to get the best out of the real specialists

- Leadership and decision-making skills
- The ability to plan and forecast
- And to actually get things done!

In fact – the very stuff of future senior management!

Management must understand that effective communication with stakeholders must be an integral part of the project plan

Nevertheless, project management should not be instituted until the leaders of the organization:[9]

- Understand what it entails

- Are genuinely committed to its use, and

- Are willing and able to develop a suitable culture for project management to germinate and grow

Realizing the benefits of a project requires special attention, especially those that impact a large number of people such as is the case with administrative changes or public infrastructure projects. Therefore, it is essential to conduct the necessary communications, explanations and, if necessary, training for those impacted. Management should realize that this must be an integral part of the project plan.

1.8   Professionalism in project work

The idea of setting out to achieve certain predetermined objectives in several concurrent areas presupposes the application of discipline and control through sound management practices. Formal projects typically require delegation of effort to various specialized groups through whom the separate project components will be achieved. At the same time, this must be matched by professional coordination to avoid the problems of fragmentation.

The more vital or urgent the endeavor and the more complex the situation, the more important it is to have the project managed by competent, effective, entrepreneurial leadership. Such leadership involves knowing what has to be done, how to do it, when to do it, and perhaps most importantly, how to deal with the people who will get it done. Such is the mark of a true professional!

So, this seems like a good place to talk about project management as a profession.

What are the attributes of a profession?

In the late 1970s and early 1980s, some members of the Project

Management Institute ("PMI") made a significant effort to develop project management into a recognized profession. By examining such callings as accounting, engineering, law, medicine and so on, a study by PMI established that there were five essential attributes generally associated with a recognized profession.[10] These are:

1. A Unique Body of Knowledge

The existence of principles and concepts unique to the particular profession that can be codified and documented so that they may be studied and learned through formal education

2. Supporting Educational Programs

That define the minimum level of entry to a recognized educational process leading to a progressive career path.

3. A Qualifying Process

For setting and promoting the standards for professional designation

4. A Code of Ethics

Making explicit what is considered to be appropriate behavior and which is used to self-police unprofessional behavior, and hence limit the necessity for direct legal intervention

5. A Supporting Organization

That acts as the self-policing agency and reflect a desire on the part of its membership to commit time, money and energy towards self-improvement, publishing research and experience to enhance the body of knowledge, and generally working towards a better understanding by the public of its existence and purpose.

In addition, members of PMI identified a number of characteristics of professional organizations.[11] A professional organization:

- Promotes public interest and awareness, and exhibits public responsibility

- Is responsive to a diverse environment

- Exhibits equity and fairness in all its dealings

- Maintains effective communications throughout its domain, and

- Cultivates a desire to belong

Project management is an established discipline and a valuable career path

Many people have asked me whether I consider project management a profession. Frankly, I don't think so, at least not in the sense of the established professions such as the legal, accounting and medical professions. These have been around for centuries and are well-established in people's minds as "The Professions".

Even corporate management, which has been around for over a century, has only recently seen the launch of the Chartered Management Institute in the UK (2002). Only now may its members consider themselves "Professionals" (with a capital "P").

Personally, I think the question of whether or not project management is a formal profession is a side issue. Project management is, without a doubt, an established discipline in its own right, a valuable career path, and it should be pursued with all the management professionalism that individuals can muster.

1.9   The Need for a Project Management Body of Knowledge

From the list of attributes of a profession in the previous section, you will see that a relevant body of knowledge (we'll call it a PM-BoK), is the number-one building block to forming the basis for conducting ourselves professionally. A defined, published, and accepted body of knowledge reflecting good practice is essential for the development of certification and competency examinations. It also serves to define what should be taught in formal educational programs, as well as serve as criteria for evaluating such programs for accreditation purposes.

But the world of project management application is still developing rapidly and its practice is still evolving. That is good news for its practitioners. However, while codification is a good idea, we must beware of concepts and ideas that get "institutionalized" to the extent of inflexibility, or become regimented and obsolete.

In short, the development of a PMBoK is a journey, not a destination. It is initially generic in nature, and its intent is to provide a common basis for understanding the "mechanics" of project management across all areas of application, in all industries and in all cultural regimes. Moreover, it should cover all topics needed to understand and manage projects successfully.

References

[1] You can find details of the SCOPE-PAK approach to project planning at http://www.maxwideman.com/papers/scopepak/intro.htm

[2] Barnes, M., Abstracted from text, Martin Barnes Project Management, UK, 1988

[3] Jenett, E., some observations since updated and expanded from About Project Management, PMnetwork, PA: Project Management Institute, January 1991, p53

[4] Cleland, D.I., commentary to H. Padgham on "strategic issues for PMI", December 7, 1990

[5] Obeng, Dr. E., Project Managers Can Show the Way, The Sunday Times, November 18, 1990, Section 6

[6] Cooke-Davies, T., Abstracted from Return of the Project Managers, Management Today, British Institute of Management (UK), May 1990

[7] PMI-INTERNET Agreement dated October 16,1990, p3

[8] Humphreys, A.S., Business Planning and Development, Report, British Institute of Management (UK), June 1986, p81

[9] Cleland, D.I., Project Management: Strategic Design and Implementation, PA: Tab Books, Inc., 1990, p53

[10] Studies conducted under the direction of Dr. John Adams (then) Project Management Institute Director of Education, and presented to the Project Management Institute's Board c. 1982, Project Management Quarterly, Dec. 1982, p8; Project Management Journal, Aug. 1986, p15; Project Management Body of Knowledge, March 28, 1987 p0-1

[11] Minutes of Special Organizational Development Project meeting for the Project Management Institute held January 27, 1989

CHAPTER 2

Defining project, program and portfolio management

2.1 What is a project?

In the English language, the word "project" has become common-place and is frequently used for anything that matches our vague understanding of the word. For example, the baking of a pie can be viewed and undertaken as a "project" because it has all the ingredients (literally!) of a project, as shown in Figure 2-1. But when you come to think of it, a project is only really a project if you decide to make it so – and manage the activities as such. Otherwise, all you have embarked upon is simply a "voyage of discovery"!

INPUTS   X   TOOLS & TECHNIQUES   =   OUTPUTS

Figure 2-1: The pie making project[1]

Actually, the word "project" seems to have several meanings, from association with a plan, scheme or undertaking for accomplishing a purpose to the actual purpose itself. How many times have you seen someone point to something and declare with pride: "That was one of my projects!" Does that mean they are referring to the object that now exists, or to the exercise of creating it?

So, before we go anywhere, we must agree on what a project really is. Definitions of "project" in the project management literature are many and various. These are often composed to suit the specific environment envisaged by the author, so there is no universally accepted wording. Indeed, my Glossary currently lists more than twenty.[2] Here are several examples from respected authors.

A project is:

- A temporary endeavor undertaken to create a unique product or service.[3]

"Project" means different things to different people

- A unique set of coordinated activities, with definite starting and finishing points, undertaken by an individual or organization to meet specific objectives within a defined schedule of cost and performance parameters.[4]

- An endeavor in which human, material and financial resources are organized in a novel way, to undertake a unique scope of work of given specification, within constraints of cost and time, so as to achieve unitary, beneficial change, through delivery of quantified and qualitative objectives.[5]

- A temporary organization in a management environment created for the purpose of delivering one or more business products according to a specified business case. A project is a finite process with a definite start and end. Projects always need to be managed in order to be successful.[6]

- A unique, novel and transient endeavor undertaken to achieve novel objectives and involving considerable risk and uncertainty.[7]

2.2   What can we conclude from our sample of definitions?

Some of the foregoing definitions might be criticized for being incomplete, but collectively we can get a good sense of what a project embraces. All of them seem to be saying that what we are looking at is a group of activities with some focus. All that tells us is what we can expect to find in a project and not necessarily what a project actually is.

A project is a means to an end

A project is a means to an end. It can therefore apply to any effort or assignment that will end when a goal is reached. The essential point is that a project is not a permanent or long-term activity. Rather, it is any endeavor especially set up and ending with a specific, unique or infrequent accomplishment, end result or product. This is the distinguishing characteristic of a project, and this lays the foundation for the whole of project management.

Today we have a better understanding of what we mean by *project*, especially since the publication of Peter Senge's erudite treatise on what he calls "The Fifth Discipline".[8] This work explains many phenomena in terms of graphical models or **systems**. We will develop this thought further in chapter 7 and present some models of our own to illustrate the point.

All projects have an unequivocal and formal goal orientation and a finite life span

In practice, all projects have an unequivocal and formal goal orientation and a finite life span. That is to say, since a project is established to achieve a predetermined result, it has specific start and end points.[9] It is also true that the work to be accomplished is typically constrained by the limited availability of necessary resources.

Suffice it to say that a project can be viewed as a system with inputs and outputs. Indeed, it is a system for accomplishing an objective, one that encompasses all of the complexities that a project typically involves, such as we described under "Special features" in chapter 1. Although it is a simple concept, it can lead to a dramatically different management environment, as we'll see. It means the difference between maintaining an ongoing business and the excitement and challenges of creating something new!

So in summary and for our purposes, we might characterize a project as:

Projects are not limited by field of activity, size or duration

A novel undertaking and systematic process to create a new product or service, or upgrading of an existing one, the delivery of which signals completion. Projects involve risk and are typically constrained by limited resources.

We should point out here that projects are not limited to any particular field of activity, such as administration, information technology or construction, though the latter may be the largest and longest. Nor is there any limitation on size or duration. In fact, projects embrace all kinds of opportunities as we saw from the list under "Who is project management really for?" in chapter 1. We should also stop and observe that our definition does not describe how the project's objectives are to be achieved. This is explained in the definition of project management itself.

2.3   What is project management?

Now that we know what a project is, we could say that project management is just the management of the system that represents a project. On this basis, the following simple definitions might be sufficient:

The art of making things happen.[10]

Or

The discipline of managing projects successfully.[11]

But that is where simplicity ends. The business of selecting, coordinating and managing all the system inputs and validating and verifying the outputs are anything but simple. Even then we might not have a successful project unless we've taken into account all of the people's interests involved. Here again various respected authors have proposed a variety of definitions.

Project Management is:

- The application of knowledge, skills, tools, and techniques to project activities to meet project requirements.[12]

- The combination of systems, techniques, and people required to complete a project within established goals of time, budget, and quality.[13]

The notion of "on time, on budget" is no longer sufficient for today's projects

- The art of directing and coordinating human and material resources throughout the life of a project by using modern management techniques to achieve predetermined objectives of scope, quality, time and cost, and participant satisfaction.[14]

- The discipline of managing projects successfully. Project management can and should be applied throughout the project lifecycle, from the earliest stages of concept definition into operations & maintenance. It comprises the management of all that is involved in achieving the project objectives safely and within agreed time, cost, technical, quality and other performance criteria. Project management provides the *single point of integrative responsibility* needed to ensure that everything on the project is managed effectively to ensure a successful project deliverable.[15]

Note that the old notion of project management just being *on time and in budget* is no longer sufficient. Today we live in a world that now expects much more from the project management discipline.

First of all, project management is probably just as much an art as it is a science. Secondly, as well as balancing the four core constraints of scope, quality, time and cost, we must recognize the more abstruse values that make a project successful. These include customer satisfaction and the product's potential to deliver benefit or value to justify the project's cost. Certainly emphasis should be on *customer* satisfaction – as these people are the most significant participants in terms of assessing project success.

Project management is both an art and a science with a focus on customer satsifaction

Thirdly, and by no means least, projects take place in a risk-prone environment. This environment must be assessed and managed carefully, and steps taken to mitigate the most obvious risks. It also implies that project management involves pre-emptive planning. Indeed, these are perhaps the most significant responsibilities of the project manager.

Once again for our purposes we might characterize project management as:

> The art and science of managing a project from inception to closure as evidenced by successful product delivery and transfer.[16]

Of course, this does beg the question of what do we mean by success? This is a major area of discussion in itself and we'll devote the whole of chapter 15 to this subject.

2.4   What about program management?

Some people are involved in programs, or program management, and once again there is a diversity of views as to the exact meaning of these terms. For many years and for some organizations, the terms program management and project management were, and still are, synonymous. In many cases, there is some justification for this because many of the tools and techniques are largely the same even though the complexity of their application in a program is much greater. Once again it is worth examining the literature for a selection of definitions.

Program management is:

- A group of related projects managed in a coordinated way. Programs usually include an element of ongoing work.[17]

- The management of a related series of projects executed over a broad period of time, and which are designed to accomplish broad goals, to which the individual projects contribute.[18]

- The overall direction of a project portfolio. It includes project prioritization, funding, support, and other management functions.[19]

- A specific undertaking to achieve a number of objectives. Examples include product and economic development programs where the programs follow a concept/design life cycle before moving into the implementation of multiple projects or production units. In the case of multiple projects there is not the same common objective. Instead, each project follows its own project lifecycle but the set of lifecycles should be coordinated and managed so the overall system works effectively.[20]

The definition of program management is ambivalent but project portfolio management is quite distinct

So, for our purposes we can summarize program management as:

The effective management of a program that may cover any or all of the following:[21]

- A portfolio of projects related to some common objective
- An organization's business strategy which is to be implemented through projects
- The interdependencies between a number of projects
- Resource allocation amongst a portfolio of projects

Before we move on to portfolio management, however, let us first agree on what if any is the difference between project management and program management. We can start from the premise that a program is made up of a number of projects, all with a common purpose, but possibly phased in progressively, either because of interdependencies, or for purposes of leveling resources. However, we could establish exactly the same scenario simply by recognizing the entire endeavor as one very large project and the lesser components equivalent to subprojects.

In a similar way, on a complex public building project as an example, many pieces of the work are subcontracted out, and the leaders of these subcomponents are often given the title of project manager. From their perspective, their subcontract is their entire project. So, it is not unusual to see multiple hard hats floating round the site each carrying the label project manager. Does that make the whole building project a program?

In such cases it appears that the only difference is one of scale, labeling and the preferences of the sponsoring organization.

2.5   Portfolio management

Portfolio management is the latest area of interest to attract project management attention. In the project context, a portfolio is clearly a group of projects, but they may or may not be of a common type and may or may not have a common objective other than serving the enterprise's overall goals.

In the Guide to the PMBOK, under the heading of related endeavors, project portfolio management receives a brief mention as follows:[22]

- Project portfolio management refers to the selection and support of projects or program investments. The organization's strategic plan and available resources guide these investments in projects and programs

Other authors apparently see it differently. For example, portfolio management is:

Project portfolio management is the responsibility of corporate management

- The management of a number of projects that do not share a common objective. For example, the responsibility of an operations manager of a company managing several different projects for different clients.[23]

I believe that the eventual definition will settle down around a high-level corporate management responsibility for selecting and orchestrating a group of projects that may or may not be of a similar type, e.g., a mix of research and development, information technology and facility projects. The essential feature of portfolio management will be to ensure that the total projects managed:

- All add value to the enterprise

- Are selected and conducted within the capacity of the enterprise, and

- Have responsibility assigned to someone for ensuring that the benefits from each are realized

As such, portfolio management may fall within the domain of project management, but is a senior corporate management responsibility and therefore is beyond the responsibility of the individual project manager.

We will explore project portfolio management in chapters 13 and 14.

2.6   What can you conclude from these definitions?

If there is one thing that you can conclude from these definitions, it is that nothing is clear-cut and simple. So whether you are learning from your instructor, taking instructions from your boss, giving instructions to your team, reading or even writing a book on project management, make sure that the major definitions you use are clearly defined, accurate and suited to your purpose.

References

[1] Giammalvo P.D., contributed by Email 7/27/04

[2] See http://www.maxwideman.com/pmglossary/PMG_P09.htm#Project%20Boundary

[3] Glossary in *A Guide to the Project Management Body of Knowledge*, 2000 Edition, PA: Project Management Institute, 2000, p204

[4] British Standard BS6079, 1996

[5] Turner, J.R., *The Handbook of Project Based Management: Improving Processes for Achieving Your Strategic Objectives*, 1992

[6] PRINCE2 *Reference Manual*, Office of Government Commerce, London, UK, 2002

[7] Turner, R. Interpreted from the Gower Handbook of Project Management, 3rd. Edn, Ch 1

[8] Senge, P.M., *The Fifth Discipline: The Art and Practice of the Learning Organization*, Doubleday, NY, 1990. An even more useful one followed this work: *The Fifth Discipline: Fieldbook*, Doubleday, NY, 1994.

[9] Ahmed, M., D. Alderman, *Project Management: A Management Accounting Perspective*, The Society of Management Accountants of Canada, Hamilton, Ontario, 1986, pp1 and 2

[10] Bibby, J., in presentation material, 1979.

[11] Patel, M.B., & P.W.G. Morris. Centre for Research in the Management of Projects (CRMP), University of Manchester, UK, 1999

[12] Glossary in *A Guide to the Project Management Body of Knowledge*, 2000 Edition, Project Management Institute, 2000, p205

[13] Baker, S & K. Baker. *On Time/On Budget*, Prentice Hall, Englewood Cliffs, NJ, 1992

[14] PMBOK March 28, 1987, p4-1

[15] Patel, M.B., & P.W.G. Morris. Centre for Research in the Management of Projects (CRMP), University of Manchester, UK, 1999

[16] Project Management Information System (BC Government Project), 1997

[17] Glossary in *A Guide to the Project Management Body of Knowledge*, 2000 Edition, Project Management Institute, 2000, p204

[18] Glossary in PMBOK March 28, 1987

[19] Mooz, H., K. Forsberg, & H. Cotterham, *Communicating Project Management*, John Wiley & Sons, 2003, Ch5

[20] Projectnet Glossary, April 1997, on the web site of the UK publication Project Manager Today

[21] Patel, M.B., & P.W.G. Morris. Centre for Research in the Management of Projects (CRMP), University of Manchester, UK, 1999

[22] *A Guide to the Project Management Body of Knowledge*, PA: Project Management Institute, 2000 Edition, p10

[23] Patel, M.B., & P.W.G. Morris, draft papers, Centre for Research in the Management of Projects (CRMP), UK: University of Manchester, 1999

CHAPTER 3

Project management content

3.1   An illustration is worth a thousand words

One of the earliest illustrations of project management content and its focus on success is shown in Figure 3-1.

In the figure, the four core management functions of scope, quality, time and cost, represent the project objectives (as viewed by the project's sponsor) or constraints (as viewed by the project manager). However, the project is enabled by the facilitating management functions of human resources, contract/procurement, and information/communications. Project risk management seems to be a sort of bridging function between the two. These two sets of functions are discussed in greater detail in sections that follow.

Project success is established when the stakeholders express satisfaction with the process and the customers express satisfaction with the product

The intent of the diagram is to show that project management integrates these functions progressively through the project life span. The aim is to satisfy the stakeholders according to the project's established requirements. Project success is typically established when the stakeholders express their collective satisfaction with the process and, in particular, the customers express their satisfaction with the product.

The arrows in the diagram are intended to imply an input/output system that, in many cases, is iterative. An underlying principle in project management is first to plan and then to produce. Moreover, as suggested by the diagram, the priority sequence in planning tends to be clockwise through the diagram, while the producing sequence tends to be counterclockwise.

3.2   Is project management unique – and if so why?

Many have argued that managing a project simply requires the application of standard management methods to project-type work, that the body of knowledge is therefore the same and, consequently, there is no basis for an independent discipline. Certainly there are similarities and overlaps. However, as we noted earlier, the very definition of project leads to a dramatically different management environment. So it is useful to compare an established ongoing corporate environment with a project environment.

A well managed production or service organization is often characterized as follows:

- Roles and relationships are well understood, having been developed and adjusted over protracted periods

An established corporate environment is dramatically different from a project environment

- Tasks are generally continuous, repetitive or exhibit substantial similarity

- Relatively large quantities of goods or services are produced per given time period

- The workload tends to track external demand rather than special internal needs

- Given these conditions, there is relative stability, consequently

- Management of time is not a high priority

- If change is minimal and protracted, it can be thoroughly programmed and progressively integrated, and

- Management concerns itself with projects only on an exception basis

In summary, the work places of such enterprises are bounded by traditional hierarchies, lines of authority, centralized control and repetitive, assembly-line type jobs.

This is in marked contrast to the project environment that features:

- Temporary team work
- Informal relationships
- A complex management environment
- Specific time constraints
- Limited critical products

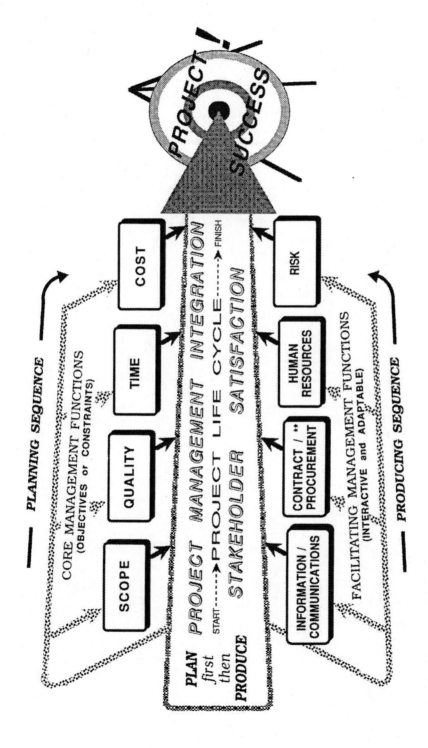

Figure 3-1: Project management integration – the source of success

- Limited and/or shared resources
- Highly variable levels of effort or work loads
- Measurable progress against plan
- Rapid change, and
- Hopefully a clear and satisfying conclusion

But perhaps the overarching difference is the fact that a project has a unique life span that we will discuss shortly.

Projects are an opportunity to gain experience

Happily, for those inclined towards project work, this is a much more exciting and challenging work environment, even though, quite frankly, it can be a career risk. When the project is done, you may well have to look for another project. On the other hand, projects represent an opportunity to gain unparalleled experience. Still, there are many who are constitutionally unsuited to project work and they should not be forced onto project teams in the interests of both themselves and their teammates if unnecessary stress and conflict is to be avoided.

The project environment is discussed in greater detail in later chapters

3.3   Project management is the management of a system

Later on we'll introduce you to a couple of models that have some interesting implications and increases our understanding. For now, we'll take a more broad-brush approach.

If projects are defined in terms of specific objectives and constraints, then their achievement is a systematic process. Therefore, it is important to recognize that when the term project management is used, it is the management of the process, and not the management of the resulting product or facility being referred to. Indeed, project management itself is a process of managing people within a project-oriented environment. Perhaps the point is, it is much more than just drawing bar charts on a computer, completing forms, and counting hours against completed tasks.

Experience has shown that where project work is concerned, traditional management hierarchies and relationships break down and, consequently, new management philosophies, strategies and relationships are required. In particular, these tend to cut across the normal flow of corporate authority and responsibility and radiate beyond any single functional unit in the organization. In addition, the life span of the project management process has some very typical and distinctive but demanding characteristics, as we'll see in the next section.

3.4   The project time frame

Projects have a start and a finish, that's the easy part. However, answering the questions "When is the start and when is the finish?" is quite another matter. There is a lot of disagreement here too, and once again it really depends on the project environment in which you are working. For our purposes we'll develop a generic time frame from first principles. But even before that, what shall we call this time frame?

You may have noted that we have been using the term "life-span" and not "life-cycle". This is a good example of the institutionalization of inappropriate terminology. The last thing we should be conveying is the idea of projects going round in circles, even if some of them unhappily do. We don't think of a person's life *cycle*, we think of their life *span*.

Management control is the true "cycle" in project management

However, there is another good reason to avoid the use of the word "cycle". A major responsibility of project management is to exercise direction and control and this is a repeated exercise of progress observation, analysis and course correction that we describe in detail in chapter 10. In the PMBOK® Guide this sequence is known as the "Controlling Processes"[1] and is indeed a true "cycle".

Unfortunately, the term "project life cycle" has become well established and if that is the label used in your organization you're probably stuck with it. Still, it is important to keep in mind the difference between the project's life span and its control cycle. In this book we will use the term "project life span" (PLS) to represent the four major sequential time periods through which every project should pass. These four periods or phases are variously named as:

1. Concept, Conception, Idea statement, Inception, Proposal

2. Definition, Development, Elaboration, Feasibility, Gestation

3. Cultivation, Execution, Construction, Design & Construction, Implementation

4. Closeout, Closure, Commissioning & transfer, Finishing, Hand over, Maturation, Transition

You will note that each of these four major phases has a number of possible different labels that we have selected from different areas of project management application. There are probably others as well and you should go with whatever is common in your field. The important point to note is that each of the four major phases has distinct and common implications and may be further broken down into stages. These stages will reflect the area of project management application and the size and complexity of the specific project.

3.5   What is an "iteration"

Before we go any further perhaps we should clarify what we mean by "iteration". In project work an iteration is:

> A distinct series of activities designed to float ideas, e.g.,
> - Samples for review, or
> - Modules and components for testing
> - Also known as prototyping, etc
>
> Which are produced, perhaps in the form of mockups, before solidifying the ideas into the final working product. The essence of iteration is to repeat the sequence to yield results successively closer to the required product.

3.6   The basis of the project life span

Project management is a management overhead and, as such, its only purpose can be to produce a more successful product than would otherwise occur had such management not been in place. In other words, it must justify its existence. Yes, we need to talk about what we mean by success, but we'll discuss that in detail in chapter 15. Meantime, if there are any principles of project management at all, the most fundamental and distinguishing of project management, is:

> **"Plan before Doing"**

You may have seen this expressed a little differently, but the intent is the same:

> **"Plan your work, work your plan"**

Needless to say, everyone should be generally satisfied with the "plan" before starting the "doing". For purposes of control at the executive management level, a checkpoint or "gate" is inserted between the two. So now we have two broad periods involving two quite different types of activities. In practical terms, these broad periods can each be subdivided into two phases. Thus, the planning period consists of a first phase in which the idea or ideas for the project are conceptualized and the value of the project ideally validated in a business case. The second phase should develop these ideas or otherwise define the details and document them in a *project charter* or *brief* for formal approval by the sponsoring or funding authority.

Two broad periods of quite different types of activities

The second major period likewise can be broken into two phases. The first of these, the third phase in our overall life span, is the actual building of the product that quite possibly includes more detailed design work. Following the creation of the product, in our final or overall fourth phase in our life span, the product must be verified to prove that it is or does what was intended. And then it must be transferred to the *care, custody and control* of the ultimate beneficiaries, typically the owners and users or customers. This general arrangement is shown in Figure 3-2 in the next section.

Another look at the four phases

You might ask: are these four phases really different and do we really need to separate them? After all, many projects just go blindly forward without noticing the difference! That is quite true and it simply means that the project is being very poorly managed. Why? Because in general:

- The activities within each phase tend to be quite distinct
- They require different levels of management attention, and
- They require different skill sets

In addition

- The transition between one phase and the next should be controlled by a *control gate*, otherwise known as an "Executive Control Point"

That is, you don't move to the next phase until you are satisfied with the current one!

In summary:

> Phase 1: Conceive an idea (*C*)
>   Sense of vision, big picture
>
> Phase 2: Develop the idea into a practical plan (*D*)
>   Listening, analysis, alignment, planning, commitment
>
> Phase 3: Execute the plan (*E*)
>   Production work, coordination, cooperation, testing
>
> Phase 4: Finish the project (*F*)
>   Transfer of product and information, review, closure

> Note that we've labeled the four phases with "*C, D, E & F*" to make them easy to remember.

3.7 Graphical depiction of the project life span

> The concept of the basic or generic project life span described above is shown in Figure 3-2.

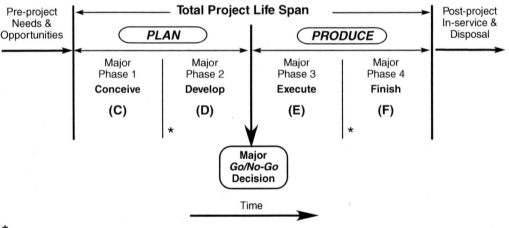

* Additional decision or approval points

Figure 3-2: The complete project life span – generic model

> As we've said, successful project management requires careful planning to precede the accomplishment of the work itself. First planning and then producing is at the heart of the modern concept. This principle in fact applies to some degree to every phase of the project. That is, planning takes place in progressively more detail

as the project progresses, but the overall project plan should be subjected to a critical review at a high level, prior to being finalized and approved for implementation. Thus, a major go/no-go decision point is established about midway through the total life span of the project, as shown in Figure 3-2. This go/no-go decision or Executive Control Point is discussed in Chapter 10, Project controls.

Project life spans must be designed to suit the particular project

Is that all there is to it? It is true that in the practical world of project management your project life spans may seem very different or much more complicated. When it comes to the detail, project life spans can be many and various, and must be designed to suit the particular project and its environment. The key is flexibility; otherwise the project can be overcome with unnecessary and unproductive bureaucracy. We'll take a look at some of the practical implications in the next chapter.

The planning work preceding the major go/no-go decision is sometimes referred to as "upstream" or "soft" phases, while the production phases following this break point are referred to as "downstream" or "hard" phases. However, this terminology is not so common these days. Nevertheless, crossing this boundary signals a major change in pace, change in the numbers and types of skills required, as well as in organizational structure. As we've already noted, the work of the first two phases is typically summarized and presented in a project charter or project brief. This provides the mechanism for formal management or sponsor approval and hence the agreed basis for monitoring and controlling the work of the subsequent phases.

3.8 The four functions representing objectives or constraints[2]

In Figure 3-1, we displayed the contents of project management that must be integrated, and noted that there are four objective functions and four facilitating functions. Let's look at these in more detail. But first, why do we call them functions? Here again there is some controversy. When they think of "functions" some people think of mathematical formulae, or they think of receptions and similar gatherings, or of officialdom. But function also means the carrying out of a particular duty and this is our intent. In other words, the work being done by project team members within their specialized project management sub-disciplines.

The four functions of scope, quality, time and cost lead to expression of the specific objectives that must not only be enunciated, but must also be compatible in the sense of being mutually achievable. The degree of compatibility may be a challenge for the project team, but if they are clearly not compatible, project management is in trouble before it even starts.

Thus, together these four functions form the frame of reference for the project, and against which the success of the project's management may be measured. From the sponsor's perspective they represent a set of requirements. From the project manager's perspective they represent limitations or constraints. Whichever way you look at it, scope, quality, time and cost are the basic parameters of project management.

Scope

A more accurate description behind the label "scope" would be "product scope". This is a description of the project's outputs, namely products or deliverables. Since the scope of a project must first be identified, developed, and then has the habit of changing during the rest of the project's life span, this gives rise to the need for *scope management.*

A description of product scope, by the way, should not be confused with a description of the scope of work, although it often is. The scope of work is a description of the work involved in creating the scope deliverables and cannot be determined until the latter have been identified.

Quality

For the products of a project to be considered satisfactory, certain standards of quality must be defined and achieved. This is known as the quality *grade* of the product and provides the baseline of reference for quality monitoring and control typically referred to as "conformance to requirements". All of this calls for *quality management.*

Time

As we've already discussed, the life of a project is finite, which is to say that the time available for completion is limited. In reality, time itself is quite inflexible, but the activities required for the project must be carefully planned and scheduled if they are to be completed within the time available. This process of planning and scheduling is referred to as ***time management.***

Cost

"Time is money" is a well-recognized catch phrase in our society, so money is closely associated with the use of time although somewhat more flexible. However, the major project costs stem from the consumption of resources to produce the project's scope. This money, identified as the project budget, needs carefully managing under the heading of ***cost management.***

3.9   The facilitating functions[3]

The three functions of human resources, contract/procurement and information/communications represent the facilitating functions, because they are the means by which the objectives of the basic or core project management functions are achieved. In addition, there is the issue of risk that seems to be a sort of bridging function between the core functions and the facilitating functions. We'll deal with risk first.

Risk

Every project exists in an uncertain environment. The obvious companion to risk is opportunity, indeed, projects are undertaken to take advantage of an opportunity and that in itself is a risk. So, the project environment is highly uncertain. Still, there are many things we can do to identify and analyze the most obvious project risks, assess their probability and level of impact, and take action to mitigate them if deemed necessary.

As an example, one of the most common risks to most projects is that of "scope creep". That is an on-going increase in the project's scope requirements without recognition of the need for corresponding increases in cost and schedule allowances. This is a reality not always appreciated by the project's stakeholders. It is up to the project manager to engage in clear communication with those responsible and ensure that the integrity of the project parameters or constraints are not compromised by such trends.

All of this is known as ***project risk management.***

Human resources

The reality is that projects are achieved through people applying their respective skills and abilities. But the number of people and their types of skill varies considerably during the course of the project and, indeed, many are required on the project for only a short length of time. Normally, there will be a project team, led by a project manager, but even the project team is required only temporarily. Often these temporary alliances take place within a traditional management organizational setting, calling for an interactive and flexible relationship.

In this temporary setting, careful attention must be given to the assembly of people, their interactions and motivation to work together effectively through a clear understanding of their respective roles and responsibilities. Moreover, when the project comes to an end, team members must be reassigned and the people concerned found other opportunities for their skills. This is officially referred to as project human resources management. However, in our view this is a rather officious and perhaps demeaning title, and we much prefer the term *people management*.

Contract/procurement

A formal agreement with an outside party is known as an "arms-length" contract

People and their skills alone are not enough. It is the willing contribution of their services that is needed for the proper conduct of the project. Services external to the organization may be purchased through an "arms length" contract, that is to say, a formal, legal, written arrangement vested in law. On many projects, materials and equipment must also be secured by contract.

The services of those within the organization, on the other hand, may have to be acquired through informal understandings. Indeed, people negotiate every day, with buyers, sellers, bosses, employees, people they work and associate with, all in order to obtain formal and informal commitments. So it is a common experience that a major portion of a project manager's time must be spent in "procuring peoples' commitment" to the project's objectives, especially on in-house projects. Procurement, by the way, is the acquisition of something (anything) for money (or equivalent), including a job that pays wages, and includes carrying that obligation to a successful conclusion.

Thus, the commitment of these goods and services to the project, as well as the administration of their conduct or delivery, whether obtained "in-house" or bought externally to the organization, fall under the heading of ***project contract/procurement management.***

Readers should be aware, however, that in many organizations, especially where all work is done in-house, the function of contract/procurement is not recognized because it is seen solely as a specialist legal activity. Instead, the idea of personal commitment is assumed as a corporate given on the grounds that this is what people are being paid for anyway. This attitude is misplaced because it:

- Takes a distinctly limited view of the need for motivation and leadership, especially on project work, and

- Overlooks, for example, the essential skills of negotiation and dispute resolution that are a part of the procurement function

Information/communications

You can have all the other functions lined up, but I assure you that absolutely nothing happens unless there is communication. And sound, reliable information at that! Sound project management requires developing a plan, giving directions, and collecting information on the status of the work as it progresses. Further, this data is compared to the plan and, if necessary, the direction appropriately re-charted as corrective action.

On a large public project, a public relations/ information office is a good idea

Obviously, this only works if people know and understand the plan and any subsequent updates, and provide the necessary feedback. Often this feedback comes from sources both internal and external to the project, and can only be fully understood through a proper interpretation of the project environment. But not only team members need to be kept informed but all the other project's stakeholders as well. Indeed, on a large public project, there may be a project public relations office dedicated to this responsibility. Then there is the usual project obligation to maintain proper records and produce reports.

All of these activities fall under the heading of ***project information/ communications management***

3.10 The order in which the functions should be listed is significant[4]

There is a logic behind the proper sequence in listing the functions we've just discussed. Unfortunately, few seem to adhere to this sequence and that simply underlines the lack of understanding of how a project is managed.

The logical sequence is as follows:

- Scope
- Quality
- Time
- Cost
- Risk
- Human Resources
- Contract/Procurement, and
- Information/Communications

What is significant about this sequence?

Ordered in this way, the functions display a dynamic relationship representing a progressive development of information during the course of project planning. That is, the information is developed moving *down* the list and is concerned with WHAT is to be managed.

We can describe the sequence more explicitly this way:

1. What are the required products of the project? – *scope*

2. Produced to what required or specified standards? – *quality grade*

3. How long have we got? – *time*

4. How much will all this cost? – *cost*

5. How certain are we of the outcome? – *risk*

6. What is the quality of human skills required to achieve it? – *quality conformance*

7. What kind of people are needed? – *human resources*

8. What commitments must be made or what resources procured? – *contract/procurement*

9. How do we get everyone to do what they are supposed to do? – *information/communications*

Note the connections. For example, you cannot estimate a reasonable cost of the work unless you know how much time you have and the consequent speed or pace that needs to be set. Fast-paced or slow-paced jobs are both more expensive than an optimally paced job. You cannot tell if the time is going to be adequate unless you know the quality standards being set. A "highly-crafted" product is going to take longer and be more expensive than a "cheap" one. And, of course, you don't know anything at all until you know what it is that you are to produce in the first place!

Managing project implementation

In converse to the foregoing, in the course of project implementation the issue is HOW the work is to be managed. That is, you actively control the project by moving sequentially *up* the list. First, you establish effective communication with people to get them to do something and refer to the contract or other form of commitment for the agreed upon details. The type of people available or assigned must do the work, and this applies to the executives and line managers as well as members of the project team. They need to use their skills to move the project forward and, as noted above, the quality of their performance will determine the quality of the product, and so on.

Quality spans both the hard and soft sides of project management, i.e., the quality of the product and the quality of the process

And so we see that the first four functions are the traditional, well-defined passive components of project management. They are usually well documented and may be said to be "hard", i.e., scope and quality by requirements and specifications, time by schedules and charts, and cost by budgets, reports and analyses. Time and cost are perhaps the "harder" or more quantifiable by virtue of having a mathematical base. The last four, while they can be the subjects of documentation, require personal interaction and may be said to be the "soft" side of project management. These tend to depend on the social sciences, and make a great deal of use of management theory.

Note that quality spans both the hard and soft sides. Quality grade focuses on the quality of the product. However, quality in the sense of conformance to requirements focuses on the quality of performance by the people to meet that quality grade.

The correct project management integration of all these various activities required to produce the end product will together and in large measure determine the success of the project.

3.11   A word about work

For many, schedule, cost and technical performance form the three sides of a triangle, sometimes referred to as the "iron triangle" or "triple constraint". However, this falls short in representing the complete picture. Technical performance is in fact the composite of two separate variables, scope and quality. In a perceptive paper, Walter Wawruck states that scope must also be seen as distinct from work for effective management control. The paper defines project scope as: [5]

> "The bounded set of verifiable end products, or outputs which the project team undertakes to provide to the client (the owner or sponsor) of the project [or, more simply,] the required set of end results or products with specified physical and functional characteristics, i.e., the outputs."

Work changes are the responsibility of the project manager but scope changes are the responsibility of the project sponsor

> "This definition provides a clear standard against which the performance of the project can be measured. This is because it differentiates between the constraint applied by the project sponsor, and the work necessary to accomplish the project objectives, the means, methods, and management plans for which should be at the discretion of the project manager. While scope changes will still lead to changes in the work, it provides the means for distinguishing between *scope changes* that are properly the responsibility of the project's sponsor, [and] *work changes*, [that are] only the responsibility of the project manager. Of course, any change in the work approved and mandated by the project sponsor (for whatever reason even though it does not change the end products) becomes a change to the contract between the parties."

The Portland paper goes on to say that:

> "Achieving the right results, in other words, fulfilling the scope objective, is the primary test of effective performance by project management. It takes precedence over the constraints of deadlines and budgets. Failure to manage and control this aspect of the objectives (i.e., scope) is a principal reason why projects fail."

Work, on the other hand, is an integrator providing linkages between each of the project management functions, as shown in Fig-

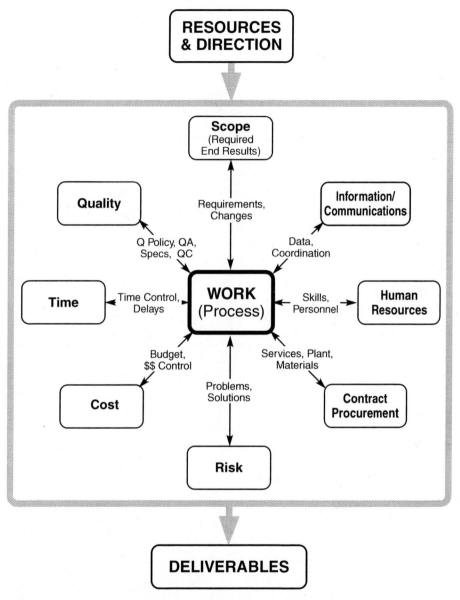

Figure 3-3: Work as an integrator

ure 3-3. In this diagram:[6]

- *Scope* determines the outputs that work must achieve during the project and each phase of it

- *Quality* defines, assures and controls the quality standards of the work

- *Time* plans, schedules and controls the progress of the work

- *Cost* budgets, estimates and controls the cost of the work

- *Risk* anticipates and controls the uncertainties involved in performing the work

Technology management is not the same as project management, but both must be closely integrated

- *Human Resources* organizes and motivates the project team and others to do the work

- *Contracts* (external and internal to the project team) defines who is to supervise and implement the work and administer the work contracted for

- *Communications* provides the necessary data for planning, coordinating and undertaking the work

Drawing a clear distinction between scope and work, and developing a better understanding of each, is yet another example of the value of having a project management body of knowledge. Of course there are aspects common to many projects that are outside of the scope of those items listed above, those that have to do with managing the **technology** involved in the project. These must be just as carefully managed if the product is to be successful. However, this aspect is always application specific and is beyond the scope of this book.

References

[1] *A Guide to the Project Management Body of Knowledge*, PA: Project Management Institute, 2000, p36

[2] Project Management Body of Knowledge, PA: Project Management Institute, March 28, 1987, p1-2

[3] Ibid., p1-3

[4] Nunn, P., Project Management Journal, PA: Project Management Institute, Aug. 1986, p105-108

[5] Wawruck, W.W., *Managing the Scope: A neglected Dimension of Effective Performance on Diverse Projects*, PMI Northwest Regional Symposium, Portland, Oregon, 1987, p202

[6] Quaife, C., in private correspondence, January 1991

CHAPTER 4

First principles of project management

4.1   Introduction

As we shall see in Part II of this book, project management is a composite series of interrelated activities with multiple dimensions. Depending on the type and class of project this management activity can be very complex, not least because the typical project environment echoes the "fractal" form of certain seashells, as we illustrate in Figures 5-3 and 5-4 in Chapter 5. That is, a similar approach can be applied at every level and branch of the project hierarchy and only the scale changes.

Project management is like a seashell. It's the same at every level but allocation of responsibility makes it complicated

However, since each level or branch may fall under different areas of responsibility in the overall project organization, the problem of different agendas may arise and the overall goals of the project may become obscured as a result.

In the literature, there is a wealth of information describing projects in all areas of application, what was achieved, how it was achieved and how successful were the results. Similarly, there is a wealth of literature providing advice on how to do project management – and presumably do it better. Based on this experiential material, various attempts have been made to assemble "bodies of knowledge" and thereby articulate the role and content of project management.[1,2,3]

Such documents have been used in several countries for the development of individual certification and competence testing, and/or by enterprises for establishing corporate standards of practice.

In contrast, there appears to be very little content establishing basic "principles" and theories to support them. This absence suggests that the building of a project management discipline is presently based only on experiential records and opinion and not on any reasonably logical or theoretical project management specific foundation. Ideally, what is needed is a generally agreed and testable set of elemental ***principles*** of project management that provide a universal reference basis for a set of generally acceptable ***practices***. It is true that although much management science theory is applicable, there is little that focuses on the specific and unique project management environment.

Project management and corporate management are very different

To emphasize that we wish to focus on the ***founding*** principles of project management, we will use the term *first* principles. You may ask, "Do we really need a set of first principles of project management?" After all, most people seem to have managed very well without them – that is, until the trouble starts. The problem is that most projects take place in a corporate environment but the approaches to corporate management and to project management are very different. Marie Scotto has provided a compelling list of differences.[4]

Perhaps the most significant of these is that "The business community believes in understaffing which it can prove is generally good business most of the time." However, projects require contingency allowances to accommodate the inevitable extra work arising through uncertainty so the practice of starving resources is a recipe for failure. If we could point to a generally accepted set of project management principles we might be able to steer clear of this perennial problem.

But what should we include? The key appears to be whether or not the principle is universally fundamental to project success. But even the definition of success is controversial. We focus more closely on success in Chapter 15, but for now we will define it as follows.

Project Success

Project success is a multi-dimensional construct

A multi-dimensional construct that inevitably means different things to different people.[5] It is best expressed at the beginning of a project in terms of key and measurable criteria upon which the relative success or failure of the project may be judged. For example, those that:[6]

- Meet key objectives of the project such as the business objectives of the sponsoring organization, owner or user, and

- Elicit satisfaction with the project management process, i.e., that the deliverable is complete, up to standard, is on time and within budget, and

- Reflect general acceptance and satisfaction with the project's deliverable on the part of the project's customer and the majority of the project's community at some time in the future.

Project success is closely linked to opportunity and risk

Project success is closely linked to opportunity and risk. Projects by their nature are risky undertakings and some project hazards cannot be entirely avoided or mitigated even when identified. Since project success may be impacted by risk events, it follows that both opportunity and risk are necessarily shared amongst the participants. You should also note that success criteria can change with time and just because certain objectives were not achieved does not necessarily mean that the project was a failure.

Other key terms are defined in Appendix C: Glossary.

4.2   First principles described

The following principles build extensively on the work of John Bing.[7] All the principles make certain assumptions about the cultural ambience of the project's environment, one that encourages and sustains teamwork and honesty and demonstrates that:[8]

All the principles make certain assumptions about the cultural ambience

1. Everyone is working towards the same or similar project goals, whatever those might be

2. Everyone is clear and agrees on who the customer is

3. Appropriate levels of skill or experience are available as needed, and

4. Everyone wants the project to succeed

The commitment principle

- An equitable commitment between the provider of resources and the project delivery team must exist before a viable project exists.

The provider of resources (money, and/or goods and services, and general direction) is typically called the project's owner or sponsor. The project delivery team is responsible for developing appropriate strategies, plans and controls for applying the necessary skills and work to convert those resources into the required deliverables or product. An *equitable* commitment means that both parties are sufficiently knowledgeable of the undertaking, the processes involved and their associated risks, and both willingly undertake the challenge.

A project commitment must be fair and reasonable

The owner of the project must understand that even with appropriate management controls in place, there must be a sharing of the risks involved. The attributes of both parties should encompass relevant skills, including those of the technology involved, experience, dedication, commitment, tenacity and authority to ensure the project's success.

Of course every project evolves through its life span and the commitment and tradeoffs will similarly evolve. On most projects the players also change as it moves through its life span, simply to meet the changing level of effort and skills required in each phase. Nevertheless, an equitable commitment can and should exist for every phase of the project if the project is to remain viable.

The success principle

- The measures of project success, in terms of both process and product, must be defined at the beginning of the project as a basis for project management decision-making and post-project evaluation.

Doing it right is not enough. It must also be the right thing to do

It is axiomatic that the goal of project management is to be successful; otherwise the incurring of this management overhead is a valueless exercise. First and foremost, project success needs to be defined in terms of the acceptability of the project's deliverables, e.g., scope, quality, relevance to client needs, effectiveness, etc; and secondly in terms of its internal processes, e.g., time, cost, efficiency, etc. The timing of the measurement of success itself may also need specifying. Without agreement on the project's success criteria, it will not be possible to measure its ultimate success.

We believe that project success is much more than just "Doing what you set out to do". It is also about whether what you are doing is in fact the right thing to do. We believe that the ultimate goal of a project, and therefore its measure of success, should be satisfaction with the product on the part of the customer and that assumes that the customer is clearly identified.

However obvious and sensible the setting of project success criteria at the beginning of a project may seem, regretfully, it is not currently a common practice. Without defining these success criteria, how can agreement be reached on a particular project's priorities, trade-offs, the significance of changes, and the overall effectiveness and efficiency of project management post-project? For this reason, a lot of conclusions drawn from experiential material could also be very questionable.

Not everyone shares the same goals

The reality of life on many projects is that everyone on or associated with it does not have the same aspirations and goals. As a result "the project gets pulled in many different directions ... [by] ...status, pride, power, greed...".[9] In most cases, this may be a little exaggerated. But even at the most elementary level, the project owner will be interested in benefiting from the product, while the workers on the project will be interested in benefiting from the process. This makes the definition of a project's success even more important – to provide a reference baseline for the correction of divergent progress.

The tetrad trade-off principle

- The core variables of the project management process, namely: product scope, quality grade, time-to-produce and total cost-at-completion must all be mutually consistent and attainable.

Scope, quality, time and cost must be mutually consistent and attainable

This principle is an extension of both the commitment principle and the success principle. The core variables of product scope, quality grade, time-to-produce and total cost-at-completion collectively, often loosely referred to as scope, quality, time and cost, respectively, are measures of internal project management efficiency. If these variables prove not to be mutually consistent and attainable, the commitment is neither equitable nor are key success criteria likely to be met. The interrelationships of these four separate variables are somewhat similar to a four-sided frame with flexible joints. One side can be secured and another moved, but only by affecting the other two.

The merit of viewing the four as a tetrad rather than selecting only three to form a triangle is that it gives greater prominence to quality. Of the four, the quality of the product is obviously the most enduring.

The strategy principle

- A strategy encompassing first planning then doing, in a focused set of sequential and progressive phases, must be in place.

The genesis of the project life span process, in its most basic form, is

How the project life span is structured is vital to project success

to be found in the very term "project management" itself. A project has, by definition, a start and a finish. The essence of management is to "plan" before "doing". Hence the most fundamental project life span process consists of four sequential periods of "start", "plan", "do" and "finish". Of course these four periods can be expanded into separate phases each with their own interim deliverables and "executive control points" (or "emergency exit ramps".) These can be designed to suit the control requirements of every type of project in every area of project management application. Indeed, this sequence is, in effect, equally applicable at every level and branch of the project organization. It is also just as relevant whether a "fast-track" strategy or an iterative approach is adopted.

The importance of this life span process and its influence on the management of the project cannot be over emphasized. This relatively short-term life-to-death environment, and the consequences that flow, is probably the only thing that uniquely distinguishes projects from non-projects.[10]

The management principle

- Policies and procedures that are effective and efficient must be in place for the proper conduct and control of the project commitment.

Who and how must also be decided

This principle is an extension of the "Strategy principle". The Strategy Principle determines what is going to be done and when. The Management Principle establishes *how* it is going to be done and *who* will do it. The attributes of this management control encompass the project's assumptions, its justification and a reference baseline in each of the core variables as a basis for progress measurement, comparison and course adjustment. The attributes of good policies and procedures encompass clear roles and responsibilities, delegation of authority, and processes for maintaining quality, time and cost, etc. as well as managing changes in the product scope and/or scope of work.

The single-point responsibility principle

- A single channel of communication must exist between the project sponsor and the project team leader for all decisions affecting the product scope.

This principle is an extension of the management principle and is necessary for effective and efficient administration of the project commitment.

Single-point responsibility must not interfere with free exchange of information

For example, the owner of the eventual product, if represented by more than one person, must nevertheless speak with one voice through a primary representative with access to the sponsor's resources. Similarly, the project's delivery team must always have a primary representative. However, this only applies to the decisions affecting the product scope and hence the project's overall cost and schedule. In all other respects, free and transparent communication is indispensable for the coordination of a complex set of project activities. Therefore, this principle must not in any way inhibit the proper exchange of information through the network of project communication channels that is required to integrate all aspects of the project.

The cultural environment principle

- Management must provide an informed and supportive cultural environment to ensure that the project delivery team is able to work to the limits of their capacity.

Corporate managements tend to place obstacles in the way of project progress

The ability of a project delivery team to produce results both effectively and efficiently is highly dependent upon the cultural environment. This cultural environment encompasses both internal and external project relations and values.[11] Internally, the management style of the team leader must be suited to the type of project and its phase in the project life span. Externally, the management of the organization in which the project takes place must be supportive and the environment free of obstacles.

Unfortunately, the reality in many organizations is that many managements place obstacles in the way of project progress, perhaps unwittingly because of management's functional heritage. This is yet another argument in favor of establishing a generally accepted set of solid project management first principles.

More description and discussion of *The First Principles of Project Management* can be found at http://www.maxwideman.com/papers/principles/intro.htm

References

[1] *A Guide to the Project Management Body of Knowledge*, PA: Project Management Institute, 1996 Edition

[2] *IPMA Competence Baseline*, International Project Management Association, Germany, 1998

[3] *CRMP Guide to the Project Management Body of Knowledge*, Centre for Research in the Management of Projects, UK: University of Manchester, 1999

[4] Scotto, M., *Project Resource Planning*, in *Project Management Handbook*, CA: Jossey-Bass, 1998, Chapter 13

[5] Shenhar, A.J., D. Dvir and O. Levy, *Project Success: A Multidimensional Strategic Concept*, research paper, MN: University of Minnesota, June 1995

[6] A composite of ideas reflected in various success factors and indicators quoted in the *Wideman Comparative Glossary of Common Project Management Terms* at http://www.maxwideman.com/pmglossary/index.htm

[7] Bing, J.A., *Principles of Project Management*, PMnetwork, PA: Project Management Institute, February 1994, p38

[8] Neal, G., by Email, 9/23/99

[9] Ibid.

[10] Section 60 *Life Cycle Design and Management, CRMP Guide to the Project Management Body of Knowledge*, Centre for Research in the Management of Projects, UK: University of Manchester, 1999

[11] For definitions of 'culture' and 'environment' in the project context, refer to the Wideman Comparative Glossary of Common Project Management Terms, see Note 6 above

Part II *Project Structure*

CHAPTER 5

The project life span

5.1 Details of the project life span and its hierarchy

The project life span (PLS) is a logical progression of the evolution of an idea to the production of a useful artifact through human effort and workmanship. Properly structured, the PLS also serves as a vehicle for management control as we saw in Chapter 3. The major phases should be separated by "gates" or "control points", through which the project should not pass without executive management approval. This general idea is shown in Figure 5-1.

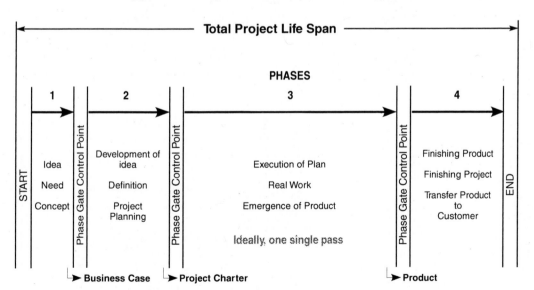

Figure 5-1: The PLS phase deliverables and executive control gates

Some will argue that the generic example I have shown is too simplistic: that probably depends on the particular type of project involved. However, too few gates, or none at all, is the reason for lack of control of many projects and their subsequent failure: too many gates, and the project becomes overwhelmed by bureaucracy and the consequent disrepute of project management.

Project management is based on "First Plan" then "Do"

As we also saw from the last chapter, the typical project time frame encompasses two sequential periods: first planning, then doing. Perhaps better terms would be "preparation and performance", or "planning and producing". We'll use the latter as they are closer to the terms we use in practice. Either way, these were further divided into four distinct major phases that are typical of the PLS of almost all areas of project management application. They are therefore considered to be generic.

Some will argue that their project life spans are not recognizable in this format. Quite possible so, but I have yet to come across any but a very few that, upon analysis, do not conform to this progression. Indeed, the high-level control of many projects could be significantly improved simply by applying this PLS discipline.

So, the generic project life span may be defined as:

Four major phases: Concept, Definition, Execution & Finish

The four sequential phases in time through which any project passes, namely: concept, definition, execution, and finishing (or phase labels with similar intent).

In the actual management of most projects, and for practical purposes, these four sequential generic phases need to be broken down into greater detail as shown in Figure 5-2.

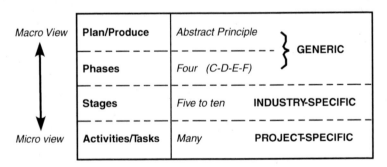

Figure 5-2: The PLS hierarchy

That is, each phase may be made up of one or more stages and, for purposes of scheduling the actual work involved, each stage is further developed into a number of activities or tasks. These activities or tasks are obviously specific to the particular project. However, it is interesting to note that the selection of appropriate stages is typically industry specific, and only the principle of "plan then produce" together with the next level of four generic phases are applicable to projects generally.

Thus, we observe from Figure 5-2 that project activities or tasks are subsets of project stages and that project stages are subsets of project phases. In other words:

- Major project phases represent the largest logical collection of activities or tasks required for high-level project control purposes

- Major project phases may be subdivided into smaller phases, especially on large projects

- Project phases are typically divided into logical project stages appropriate to the area of project management application, and

- Activities or tasks are the logical sequencing of the work in each project stage that are required to produce the product of the project. These are obviously project-specific.

Activities and tasks are subsets of project stages and project stages are subsets of project phases

The relevance and consistency of the application of project management techniques to all levels of the PLS from the macro to the micro is well worth noting. A specific task could just as well be considered as a "project" in its own right, and require the same functional considerations as the project as a whole. It is only a question of scale. A good analogy in nature is the spiral seashell, every section of which exhibits identical features but at ever decreasing scale. This phenomenon is known as a "fractal" and is illustrated in Figures 5-3 and 5-4

A "fractal" is as series of self-similar shapes of varying size. Every shape in the series is geometrically similar. Many obvious examples are found in nature such as the spiral shells of the common snail and many sea creatures. Less obvious examples include clouds, mountains, trees, river deltas, etc. The scroll casing of a hydroelectric water turbine is an engineering example. Fractals are used in mathematics to model complex natural processes.

The principles of project management apply at every level of the hierarchy. Like the snail or sea shell, every section has the same features, only the level of detail changes.

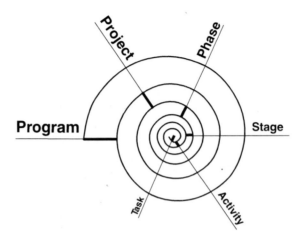

Figure 5-3: The fractal nature of project management

Figure 5-4: Sea shell showing fractal geometry

Perhaps that is why breaking the project down into manageable work packages is so attractive: it enables the same standard approach to be applied throughout. It is also why large projects tend to have multiple project managers, as we noted earlier.

5.2   Typical project phase activities

Figure 5-5 displays the typical activities we would expect to see taking place in each major phase of the generic PLS.[1] Figures 5-6 through 5-9 show the activities respectively for construction,[2] manufacturing and distribution engineering,[3] new-product-introduction/information-processing products,[4] and systems development.[5]

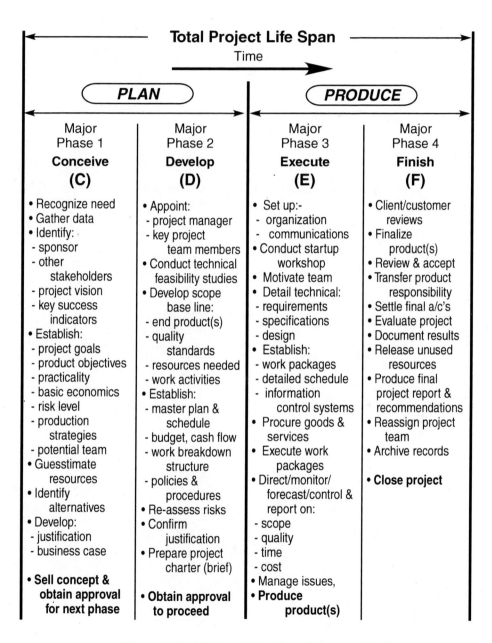

Total Project Life Span

Time

PLAN		PRODUCE	
Major Phase 1 **Conceive** **(C)**	Major Phase 2 **Develop** **(D)**	Major Phase 3 **Execute** **(E)**	Major Phase 4 **Finish** **(F)**

• Recognize need
• Gather data
• Identify:
 - sponsor
 - other
   stakeholders
 - project vision
 - key success
   indicators
• Establish:
 - project goals
 - product objectives
 - practicality
 - basic economics
 - risk level
 - production
   strategies
 - potential team
• Guesstimate
  resources
• Identify
  alternatives
• Develop:
 - justification
 - business case
 	
• **Sell concept &**
  obtain approval
  for next phase
	• Appoint:
	 - project manager
	 - key project
	   team members
	• Conduct technical
	  feasibility studies
	• Develop scope
	  base line:
	 - end product(s)
	 - quality
	   standards
	 - resources needed
	 - work activities
	• Establish:
	 - master plan &
	   schedule
	 - budget, cash flow
	 - work breakdown
	   structure
	 - policies &
	   procedures
	• Re-assess risks
	• Confirm
	  justification
	• Prepare project
	  charter (brief)
	
	• **Obtain approval**
	  to proceed
		• Set up:-
		 - organization
		 - communications
		• Conduct startup
		  workshop
		• Motivate team
		• Detail technical:
		 - requirements
		 - specifications
		 - design
		• Establish:
		 - work packages
		 - detailed schedule
		 - information
		   control systems
		• Procure goods &
		  services
		• Execute work
		  packages
		• Direct/monitor/
		  forecast/control &
		  report on:
		 - scope
		 - quality
		 - time
		 - cost
		• Manage issues,
		• **Produce**
		  product(s)
			• Client/customer
			  reviews
			• Finalize
			  product(s)
			• Review & accept
			• Transfer product
			  responsibility
			• Settle final a/c's
			• Evaluate project
			• Document results
			• Release unused
			  resources
			• Produce final
			  project report &
			  recommendations
			• Reassign project
			  team
			• Archive records
			
			• **Close project**

Figure 5-5: PLS activities by phase – typical

Note how in Figure 5-5, Phase 1: Concept results in a business case while Phase 2: Development results in a project brief or charter.

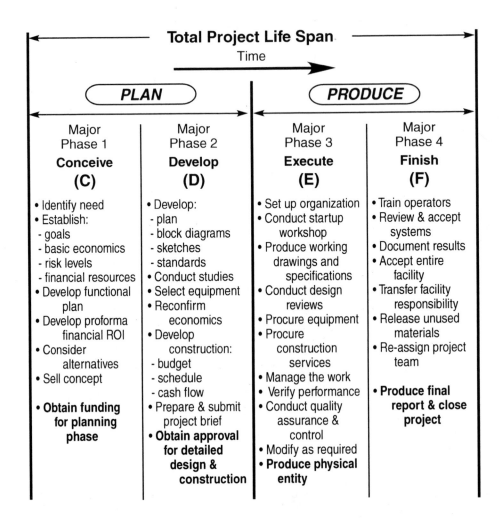

Figure 5-6: PLS activities by phase – construction

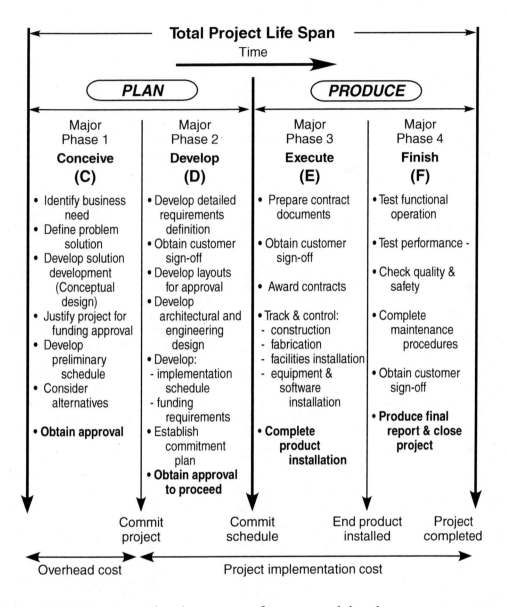

Total Project Life Span

Time

PLAN   **PRODUCE**

Major Phase 1	Major Phase 2	Major Phase 3	Major Phase 4
Conceive	**Develop**	**Execute**	**Finish**
(C)	**(D)**	**(E)**	**(F)**
• Identify business need	• Develop detailed requirements definition	• Prepare contract documents	• Test functional operation
• Define problem solution	• Obtain customer sign-off	• Obtain customer sign-off	• Test performance -
• Develop solution development (Conceptual design)	• Develop layouts for approval	• Award contracts	• Check quality & safety
• Justify project for funding approval	• Develop architectural and engineering design	• Track & control: - construction - fabrication - facilities installation - equipment & software installation	• Complete maintenance procedures
• Develop preliminary schedule	• Develop: - implementation schedule - funding requirements		• Obtain customer sign-off
• Consider alternatives	• Establish commitment plan		
• **Obtain approval**	• **Obtain approval to proceed**	• **Complete product installation**	• **Produce final report & close project**

Commit project	Commit schedule	End product installed	Project completed

Overhead cost   Project implementation cost

Figure 5-7: PLS activities by phase – manufacturing and distribution engineering

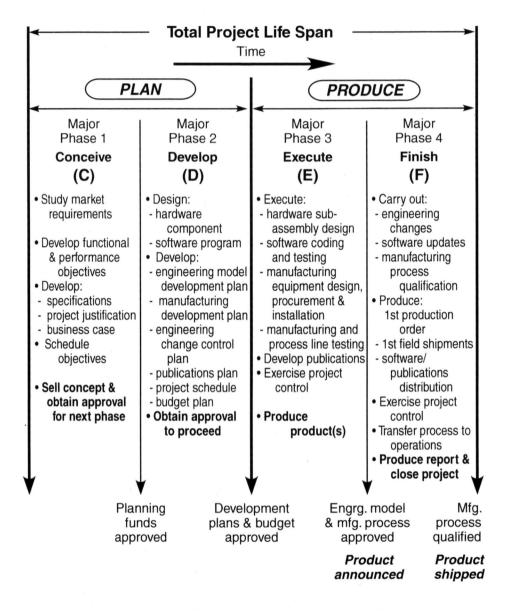

Figure 5-8: PLS activities by phase – new product introduction
or information technology products

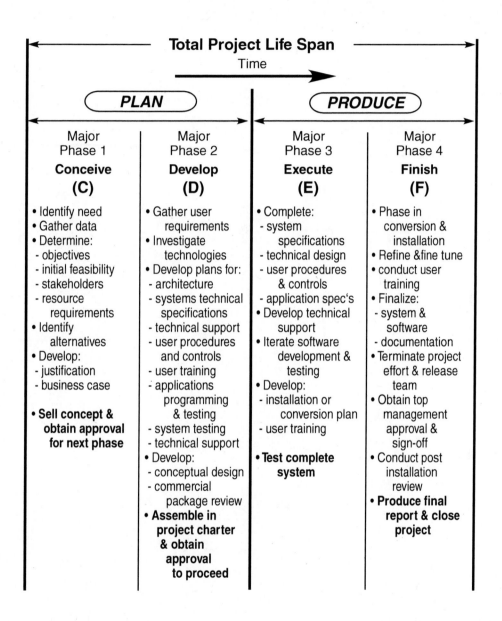

Figure 5-9: PLS activities by phase – systems development

5.3   Sample bar charts

The following simplified industry project bar charts show typical project life spans.

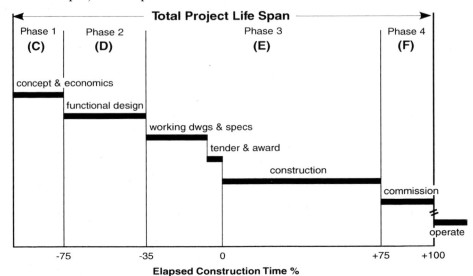

Figure 5-10: Typical construction project bar chart

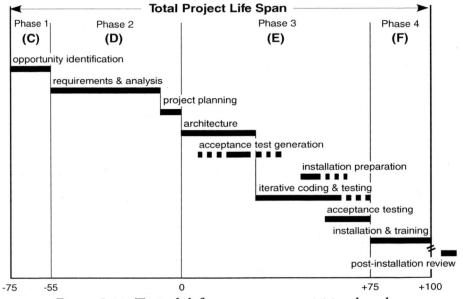

Figure 5-11: Typical defense systems acquisition bar chart

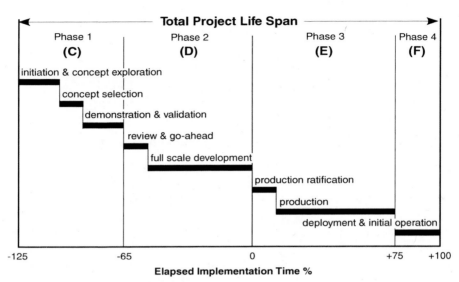

Figure 5-12: Typical information systems project bar chart

5.4 Distinctive characteristics of the PLS

One of the distinctive characteristics of project life spans, and therefore of project management, is the marked variation of some of the process features during the course of the life span. We can best explore these by presenting them graphically in the context of our standard PLS.

Level of Effort

To achieve any kind of output or product, an effort is required. But in the case of a project the relationship between effort and time is quite distinctive. To visualize this relationship, consider a curve of level-of-effort (LoE) plotted against time. Clearly, the effort starts at zero, before the project has commenced, and ends at zero, after it has been completed.

Between these two points, the time-LoE curve has a typically characteristic profile. This may be likened to a pear sliced down the middle, one half of which rests flat face downwards, with the stem at time zero. The vertical profile then exhibited is representative of the typical project's time-LoE relationship. This profile, relative to the project phases discussed earlier, is shown in Figure 5-13.

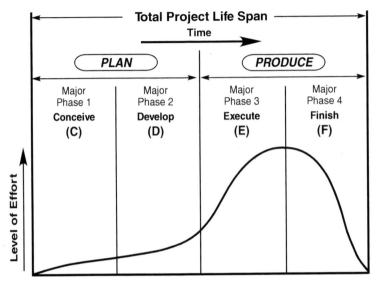

Figure 5-13: Typical PLS profile – level of effort

The "S" Curve

The pear-shaped time-LoE curve discussed in the previous section can also be plotted as a progressive cumulative total. When you do this, the result looks very much like an "S" with the bottom tail of the S at time zero, and the top tail ending at project completion. Of course, the S-curve phenomenon can be applied equally to any of the project's activities or tasks. When you set out major project activities in this way, you have a powerful control tool for assessing progress. We will return to this potential and describe *Max's rule of thumb* in a Chapter 10. A typical S-curve is shown in Figure 5-14.

Potential for adding value

The potential for adding relative and cost-effective value to the product of a project are obviously highest during the formulation or concept phase, and lowest during the finishing phase. You can also look at this as a steady reduction in "project flexibility". Between these two extremes the curve tends to follow a reverse "S" curve as shown in Figure 5-15.

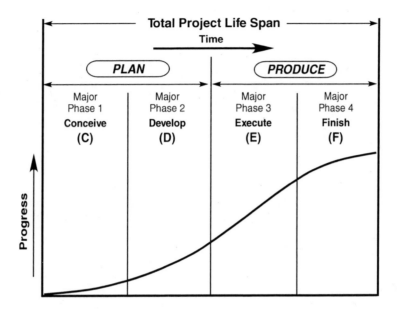

Figure 5-14: Typical PLS profile – the "S" curve

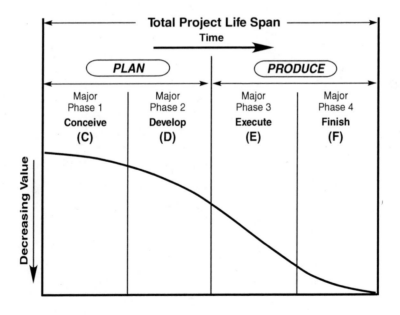

Figure 5-15: Typical PLS profile – potential for adding value

Escalating cost to change or fix

As you might expect the actual cost of making changes is least in the earliest phase of the project. However, this cost rises more and more steeply as the project progresses (Figure 5-16). In construction, for example, it has been suggested that the cost to make a change, or fix a non-conformance, increases by as much as a factor of ten in each succeeding phase. This is largely due to the increase in the number of stakeholders involved in each succeeding phase, together with the increasing amount of work that must be undone, and redone, to effect the change. To this, you should also add the increasing risk and probability of making errors in the reconfiguration, or damage to existing work.

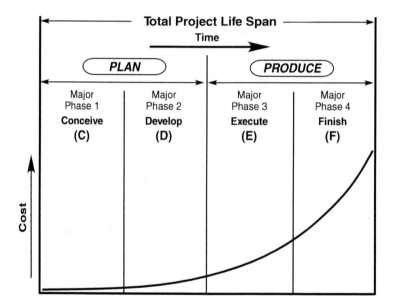

Figure 5-16: Typical PLS profile – escalating cost to change or fix

Adding value vs. cost to change

If the cost-to-change curve is superimposed on that of the potential for adding-value, the intersection of the two probably represents the point at which a constructive opportunity becomes a destructive intervention. By this I mean that before the cross-over a justifiable change adds value without being unduly disruptive of the work in progress. However, some time after the cross-over any change so disrupts the work as to negate the value of the change.

In these circumstances a necessary change should be considered as part of a new project, or at least the next upgrade (Figure 5-17).

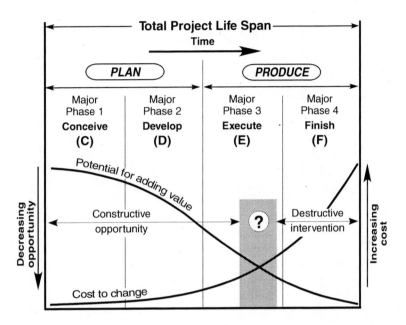

Figure 5-17: Typical PLS profile – adding value versus cost to change

Opportunity vs. amount at stake

It is instructive to compare the opportunity or risk curve with the amount at stake. In the case of a risk event, the amount at stake depends on the severity or extent of adverse consequences that could occur to the project and includes the cost of repair, recovery from lost production, and the cost of recovering from the delay to get back to where you were. However, in the simple case of significant project change or even abandonment, the amount at stake is the amount of resources already invested in the project. The cumulative curve of project investment is shown in Figure 5-18.

When we superimpose the opportunity and risk curve on the amount at stake curve we observe the following: the level of opportunity remains relatively high during the first two phases of the project. However, it does not start to fall significantly until implementation progressively eliminates further opportunities or risks of the unknowns become knowns. The amount at stake, on the other hand, is low during the first two phases, but rises rapidly during the execution phase.

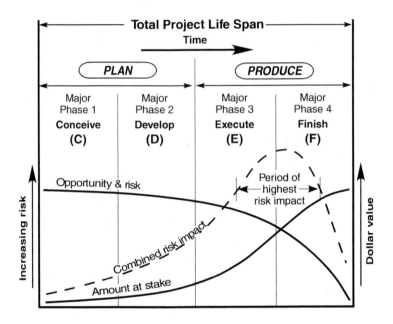

Figure 5-18: Typical PLS profile – opportunity versus amount at stake

The factoring of these two variables on a particular project can lead to some very sophisticated analysis also involving probability. However, in simplistic terms, it may be deduced from Figure 5-18 that the impact of opportunistic changes, or of risk events, is probably highest towards the end of the execution phase or at the beginning of the transfer phase as shown.

Information Explosion

The upstream phases of a project represent the development of planning information upon which the downstream production phases can be based. However, the large amount of data usually needed for the working details of execution is usually considered as work to be undertaken as an initial stage of the execution phase. This is largely because there is no point in investing in all this effort unless and until the project receives execution approval at the go/no-go decision point in the project life span.

Thus, in construction for example, the preparation of working drawings and contract documents is usually the first stage of project execution. In this short period, there is a very rapid expansion of information as shown in Figure 5-19.

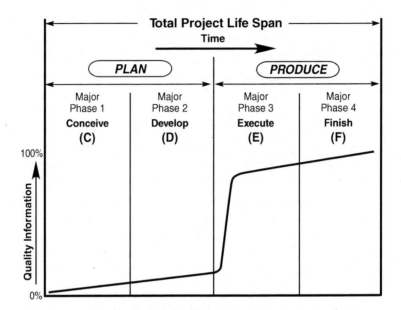

Figure 5-19: Typical PLS profile – the information explosion

5.5 Corporate/Business and Facility/Product Life Cycles

You must recognize that the project system is itself inevitably a subsystem of a larger one. This idea is illustrated in Figure 5-20

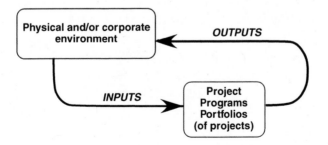

Figure 5-20: A project system is part of a larger one

In fact, there are a series of interrelated life spans as shown in Figure 5-21. According to this illustration, there is the over-arching corporate/business life span that spans the time from policy planning, through identifying needs, to disposal of the facilities, products or services of the enterprise. To the extent that parts of the corporate assets are constantly being "recycled", and that policy planning routinely occurs on an annual basis, this can be seen as a true cycle. At the next level the facility/product life cycle spans the life of specific assets, products or facilities from feasibility to disposal. By definition, the PLS covers only the period of bringing a particular facility, product or service into being.

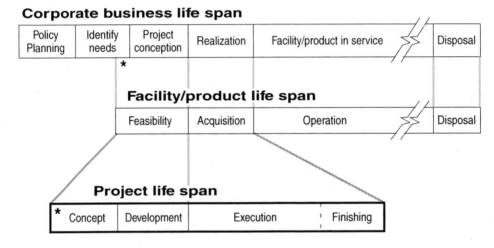

* Helping to identify the real needs in the project's
  concept phase is vital to its eventual success

Figure 5-21: Relationships with other life spans

It is worth noting, however, that the figure suggests that the PLS should start somewhat prior to the end of the "identify needs" stage of the corporate life cycle. The ideal is to include a proper needs determination within the project process itself as part of project conception. Helping your organization or sponsor to understand corporate needs is a vital part of understanding and developing the real project requirements and hence, a vital part of achieving eventual project success.

5.6   Expanding the generic project life span

As we explained at the beginning of this chapter, for practical purposes on a particular project, the generic PLS needs to be broken down into more detailed stages. As an example, Edmund Fish who works in the chemical process industry has suggested that each of the four major phases can be broken down into two or more typical stages.[6] He suggests that this is a "more robust" model because it is more immediately useful. Fish presents his model in the form of a Vee as shown in Figure 5-22.

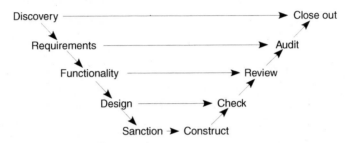

Figure 5-22: Fish's "Vee" model of the project life span

This model relates to the four-phase model as follows:

Concept Phase
- Discovery
- User requirements

Definition Phase
- Functionality
- Design
- Sanction

Execution Phase
- Construct
- Check

Finishing Phase
- Review
- Audit
- Close-out

As Fish observes in his concluding remarks:[7]

> "This model strengthens one of three essential pillars of a successful project management system, the [project life span]. Its use does not ensure project success, nor does the

failure to use it ensure project failure, but using it is likely to load the odds in your favor."

5.7   Software development is a special case

Software development, like research and development, is different because it is impossible to forecast how the product will behave until it is assembled or produced and tested

The levels of success of software development projects and perhaps information systems/technology projects generally have come in for a lot of criticism lately and are likely to continue to do so. The problem is with the difficulty of establishing a satisfactory level of project life cycle control over these types of projects. Like research and development and similar high technology projects this PLS is a special case. The reason is that it is almost impossible to forecast how software will behave until the code is assembled in increasing aggregations and given a thorough testing at each step.

If the program doesn't perform as expected, the code must be reexamined and rerun in a series of iterations. The problem lies in the difficulty of predetermining how many iterations will be needed and estimating the time required. Typically, the customer is invited to review the test runs during this iterative process – and may well decide to call for changes, adding to the difficulties. A simplified flow-chart for software development encompassing the customer's activities, the artifact's status at each stage (middle column) and the developer's activities is shown in Figure 5-23.

This process flow sequence will be familiar to software developers. However, the issue is: how does this relate to our PLS with its control gates shown earlier in Figure 5-1? In fact it is not too difficult and the comparison is shown in Figure 5-24.

When executive management imposes appropriate phase gate controls on the software development life span at the points shown, you get a satisfactory level of project control. The project manager's job is to ensure that the phase gate documentation shown in Figure 5-1 is prepared, approved by the sponsor, and thoroughly communicated to the entire project team. However, you will note that there is significant difference in phase 3. In a "traditional" construction project the ideal is a "once through only with no rework", but in software projects "multiple passes" are quite normal. This is something you must expect in software development and similar types of projects.

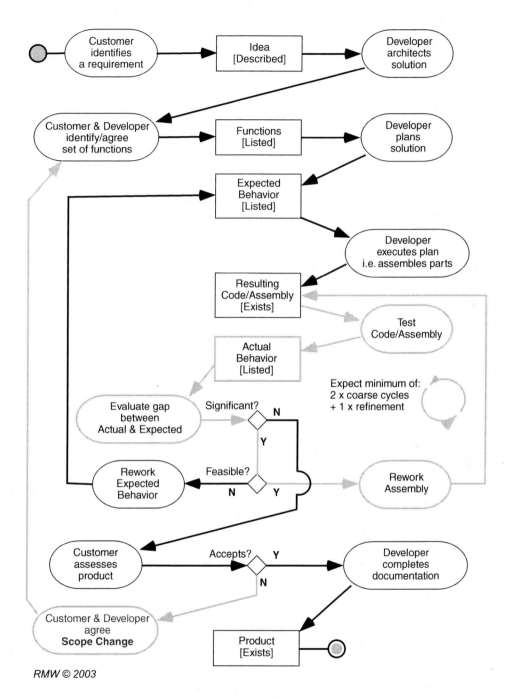

RMW © 2003

Figure 5-23: Simplified software development flow chart

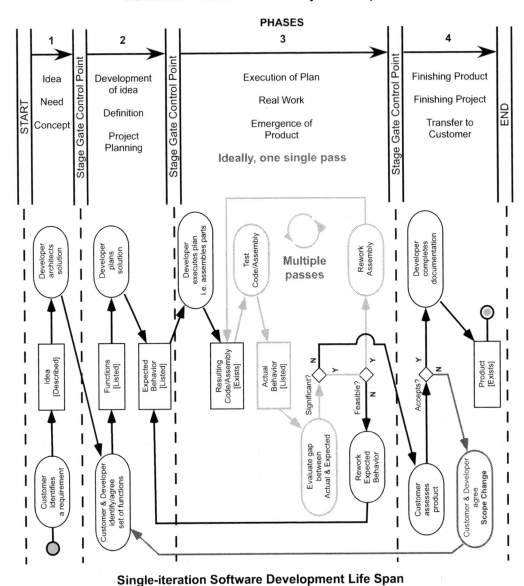

Figure 5-24: The PLS superimposed on the software development flow chart

References

[1] Project Management Body of Knowledge, PA: Project Management Institute, March 28, 1987, p1-4

[2] Wideman, R.M., *Cost Control of Capital Projects*, BC: AEW Services, 1983, p3

[3] Rogers, L.A., Project Management Journal, PA: Project Management Institute, August 1986, p109

[4] Ibid., p110

[5] Wideman, R.M., Lecture Presentation Notes, 1989

[6] Fish, E., *An Improved Project Lifecycle Model*, Pandora Consulting, http://www.maxwideman.com/guests/plc/intro.htm

[7] Ibid.

CHAPTER 6

Modeling project management

6.1 The Role of Models[1]

If we organize the knowledge we possess, then we can understand it better!

The purpose behind developing a model of the project management body of knowledge ("PMBoK"), is to help us better understand that knowledge. If we can better understand that knowledge then perhaps we can organize it so that it can be examined systematically and evaluate it as a professional discipline. It would also help universities, colleges and companies to better structure training programs, as well as conduct or propose areas for project management research. These are all necessary to advance the state-of-the-art of project management.

From the early work by the Project Management Institute("PMI") on its Ethics, Standards and Accreditation (ESA) project in the early 1980s, it was recognized that the purpose of project management is to achieve a number of concurrent objectives. As we've already discussed, these objectives are represented by scope, quality, time and cost. It was felt that each of these called for separate intellectual approaches, or represented intellectual functions, and each could be broken down into a number of topics and subtopics. For this reason, the ESA report was presented in the form of a set of work breakdown structures (WBS) to illustrate the relation and importance of the contents of each such subject area.

The work breakdown structure is the most appealing because of its simplicity

The WBS is very appealing in its simplicity, particularly to project managers who feel very comfortable with the WBS structure as a management tool. However, it is clear that the subject areas identified are themselves highly interrelated and it is difficult to visualize the nature of these relationships. In 1985, a special workshop was held at the Denver PMI seminar/symposium to review the proposed WBS model and determine whether other models might be more applicable.

In fact, the relationships between the four core functions have been the subject of considerable ongoing discussion even to this day. A number of graphic models have been proposed with a view to enhancing understanding of the project management process that could possibly lead to a more useful organization of project management knowledge. It seems that there are no "right" or "wrong" models for this purpose, although there is no question that some models facilitate the organization of the knowledge better than others.

Since modeling is central to understanding the management of the project system, and since new models are still being presented, it is worth summarizing the findings of that workshop almost twenty years ago.

6.2   Model Requirements[2]

It is important to have a sound structural framework or model of a body of knowledge to "glue all the contents together". So the purpose of the framework is to:

The framework for project management has two purposes but many goals

1. Organize and classify the knowledge content, and

2. Make certain that it is consistent.

To accomplish these goals, it was concluded that the model must:

1. Clarify the overall scope and extent of the comprehensive project management body of knowledge

2. Break up the body of knowledge into logical and understandable categories or divisions

3. Build on prior work

4. Indicate the interrelationships between the various categories into which the PMBOK can be subdivided

5. Take into account the complexities of project management and the integrating nature of the project manager's job and of his or her supporting team

6. Provide a breakdown of the PMBOK into functions covering all subject areas of project management and their processes, activities, tools and techniques

7. Be sufficiently simple and understandable to be useful (i.e., sale-able) to present and potential project management practitio-ners

8. Be consistent with the course content of PMI-sponsored project management education programs (at institutes of higher learn-ing), and

9. Be helpful to those organizations who plan to institute manag-ing by projects

"New" project management practices should be examined to make sure they are not "old" practices reinvented !

It should be emphasized that a framework or model that describes the dimensions and components of the project management body of knowledge is only a theoretical construct. It can be compre-hensive and all-inclusive, or it can be limited. It should embrace new ideas and concepts whether developed by academia or as a re-sult of new practices being developed in the field. However, "new" practices must be carefully scrutinized to ensure that they are not simply "old" practices presented with a "new twist" to become the latest short-lived "management fads", simply for promotional pur-poses.

Therefore, from the perspective of a professional discipline, only those elements that through broad application have proven them-selves, and therefore have come to be generally accepted as "good" project management, should be included. This comes down to in-cluding only those elements of theory and practice whose use has become widespread enough to support a consensus about their val-ue and usefulness. As with other professions such as law, medicine and accountancy, the "actual body of knowledge" rests with the practitioners and academics that apply and advance it.

Note that we have been careful to avoid the current popular term "best practices". Best practices are usually determined by what the majority of people are doing at the moment. However, just because every one is doing it, doesn't mean that it is the best thing or even the right thing to be doing!

6.3   PMBOK Boundaries[3]

In 1985, a select workshop group of senior consultants met in Den-ver to map out an overview of project management. This "Denver Overview" group recognized early in their discussion that there was a need to put limits or boundaries on the body of knowledge representing project management. It was also recognized that project management is a complex multi-discipline that has considerable overlap into many general management disciplines. The degree of overlap also seems to depend on the particular industrial sector, field or area of application involved. The three major points of overlap are in the areas of:

1. General management disciplines

2. The technology vested in the project in question, and

3. The supporting or service areas which are also crucial to project success

Project management overlaps other disciplines

This may be depicted by a Venn diagram in which each circle represents a particular body of knowledge and the shaded areas represent the overlaps (Figure 6-1).

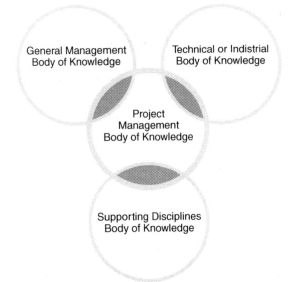

Note: The shaded areas show the overlaps with other bodies of knowledge. The boundaries are necessarily fuzzy

Figure 6-1: Scope of a project management body of knowledge

How much overlap depends on the ground-rules set to determine the scope of the PMBoK, and for this purpose it is worth examining the kinds of knowledge that are in the circles impacting project management.

6.4   Content of Related Bodies of Knowledge

It is important for project practitioners in general, and project managers in particular, to have some familiarity with the contents of the surrounding disciplines. Without this understanding they will have only limited success in carrying out their duties.

General management

While considerable controversy can be generated over what portions of the general (or business) management body of knowledge should be included in project management, there is usually little argument that the general management body of knowledge normally consists of:

You need to know more than just project management to be competent at running a project

- Business Policy
- Business Strategy
- Planning and Controlling
- Financial Management
- Accounting
- Business Economics
- Information Systems
- Organizational Behavior
- Organizational Development
- Staffing
- Personnel Development
- Marketing and Sales
- Problem Solving
- Decision Making

Supporting service disciplines

Supporting service disciplines are often essential to the success of project execution, and portions of some of the following disciplines (or service functions) should be included:

- Quality Assurance, Quality Control, Statistical Quality Control, etc.
- Configuration Management
- Logistics (Integrated Logistics Support)
- Contract Administration
- Procurement (Purchasing)
- Personnel Administration
- Facilities (Industrial) Engineering

- Legal
- Computer Programming

Technology

The body of knowledge of the technology vested in the project is somewhat more difficult to generalize since it is not necessarily represented by one circle in the Venn diagram. Frequently, on a complex project, it consists of a number of circles, each representing one of the industries, technologies, and professional areas in which project management is applied. (See Figure 7-1 in the next chaper for example.) Each has its own body of knowledge, some of which will impact in some manner on the project manager's job.

That is, project management is now used in many types of industries using complex technologies, each of which represent different disciplines. A list of typical industries is provided in Appendix B.

6.5   PMBoK Content Ground Rules

According to the 1985 Denver Overview group, an examination of Figure 6-1 suggests that the following ground rules are appropriate for scoping the project management body of knowledge:

The general PMBoK content should be limited in scope. More detailed texts are available that apply to specific areas of application

1. Much of the general management body of knowledge should be recognized as a given or prerequisite for project management and not included in the PMBoK unless aspects of this knowledge are an integral part of the project management process

2. The PMBoK should not include major areas of other disciplines, professions or detailed knowledge particular to a specific industry unless this information is also an integral part of the project management process

3. The PMBoK should not contain knowledge, technology, techniques or skills that are primarily limited to one industry or technology. That is, all items should have broad appeal in almost every area of project management application

4. The PMBoK should not include major portions of supporting or service disciplines unless they are generally applicable to most projects. Such disciplines stand on their own and are principally used as the tools of project management: only those specific applications that reinforce the job of the project management team should become part of the PMBoK

5. The PMBoK should emphasize knowledge, skills and techniques that are either unique to project management, or are fundamental to carrying out project management responsibilities

6. There is a definite need for the overlaps in the various bodies of knowledge as indicated in Figure 6-1.

In summary, project managers and their teams must have a thorough grasp of project management, some expertise in general management and a good understanding of the technology involved in their project. The potential structure and content of a typical project management function is described in Appendix A.

References

[1] Project Management Body of Knowledge, PA: Project Management Institute, March 27, 1987, pp2-1, 3-1 & 3-2

[2] Ibid., p2-3

CHAPTER 7

Project management models in three decades

7.1   Why talk about past models?

In chapters 2 and 3, we talked about the definitions of project and project management. In chapter 8 we will present a new, more sophisticated model with a new purpose. However, I believe that it will help the reader's understanding of the complexity of project management by tracing project management thinking from the age of simple models to the more complex. You should note, however, that the development of a generally accepted model of project management continues to be one of the great, unresolved issues amongst the project management community.

A generally accepted model of project management is an unresolved problem

Judging by the number of different thoughts presented in the definitions in Chapter 2, project management is clearly a complex subject and, equally clearly, there are varying opinions as to how project management should be characterized. We might take Peter Senge's advice:

The payoff could be an improvement in our way of thinking about project management

"There is something in all of us that loves to put together a puzzle, that loves to see the image of the whole emerge… Systems thinking is a discipline for seeing wholes. It is a framework for seeing interrelationships, rather than things, for seeing patterns of change rather than static 'snapshots'[1]… Ultimately, the payoff from integrating systems thinking and mental models will be not only improving our mental models (what we think) but altering our ways of thinking[2]… "

"[However,]… in some ways, [organizations] are especially vulnerable because all the individual members look to each other for standards of best practice. It may take someone from 'outside the system', such as foreign competitors, with different mental models, to finally break the spell.[3]"

7.2   Why model at all?

A model is some form of representation designed to aid in visualizing a thing that cannot be observed directly either because it has not yet been constructed or because it is abstract. There are various kinds of modeling so we must first be clear on what we mean in this case. First and foremost is the mental model – the image that forms in people's minds when a subject is discussed. Often we assume that a word or label means the same thing to all people but, as my glossary of project management terms[4] demonstrates, this is far from the case. These tacit mental models about how we see the world tend to be so deeply ingrained that they influence how we take action and even inhibit acceptance of new ideas or new models however well presented!

The words and labels we use do not mean the same thing to all people

Then there is the physical kind, such as a structural or architectural model that is a three-dimensional mock-up that may or may not be working mechanically but does demonstrate shape and physical relationships. There is also the mathematical kind, such as financial or research models, expressed as formulae that explain how certain input variables relate to an outcome variable.

But probably the most common models are diagrammatic, including charts and figures that present information by visual impression that satisfy the old saying "A picture is worth a thousand words." No doubt these are the most common because the medium, paper, is so readily available. However, they do suffer from the major drawback of being two-dimensional and various devices are often used to try to overcome this limitation.

A picture is worth a thousand words

Nevertheless, the benefits are clear. Diagrammatic models can:

- Enable each part to be identified and labeled
- Allow relationships between the parts to be identified, described and analyzed
- Simplify the complexity of real systems and enable analysis and new insights at lower cost
- Provide a common conceptual framework and thereby facilitate discussion, understanding and consensus building
- Clarify relationships, pinpoint key elements and consciously

block confused thinking

- Test the assumptions behind the model being created
- Test the impacts of different options without disrupting the real system
- Express rules and relationships more simply and so assist in their appropriate selection

Relationships between parts are more difficult to think about

- Broaden our perspective allowing people to see a larger part of the picture, if not the whole picture
- Be flexible, permitting expansion as new information comes to light
- Allow everyone to see their part without getting at cross-purposes or getting bogged down on one small part of the puzzle

Indeed, perhaps the most important aspect is the identification of relationships between the parts that might otherwise be hard to talk about. Relationships tend to be subtle and more difficult to think about and discuss and therefore tend to be the pieces that are the most valuable to understand and influence. This is particularly true of "project management" as a comprehensive discipline. If we could establish a robust model of project management that would better enable practitioners and educators alike to hold a shared vision, then we would be better positioned to establish and improve our practice, research, education and training efforts.

7.3 Project management models in the early eighties

Prior to the eighties, most of the focus was on project team behavior with only limited attention given to the organizational environment. One of the earliest models that we could find illustrated the project management construction environment (Figure 7-1).[5]

The project manager is central to a complex arrangement

This diagram illustrates the complexity of stakeholders involved or impacted by a building construction project of significant size, such as an office complex or tower. Note the central position of the project manager and his/her team. However, the project sponsor is not as well connected as the role now suggests it should be.

There have been several early attempts to illustrate the connection between cost, schedule and work, but one of the earliest attempts to diagram the relationship between the management processes of

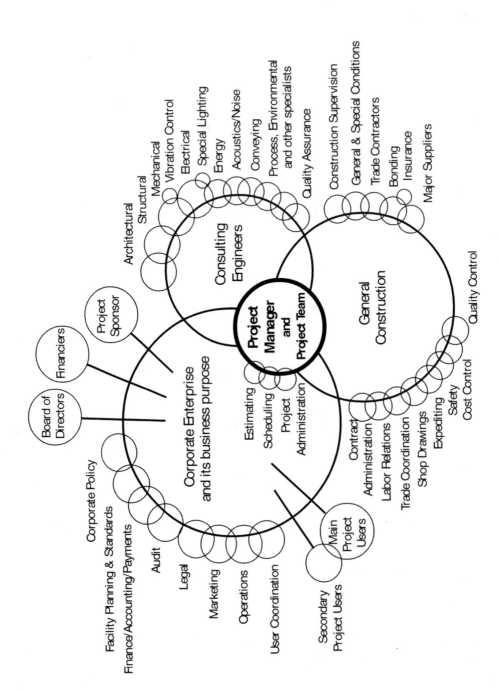

Figure 7-1: Construction project management in a corporate environment

project management appears to be my own around 1983 shown in Figure 7-2.[6]

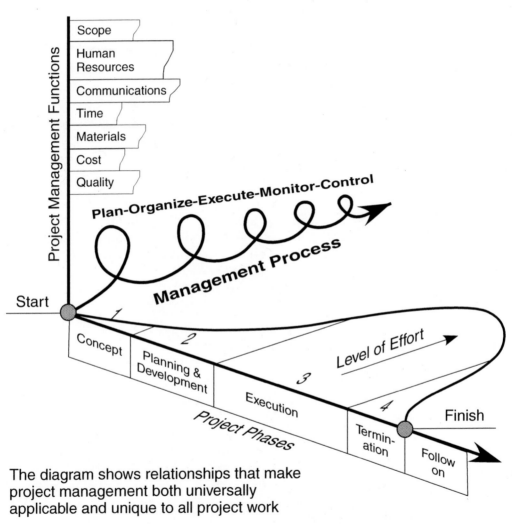

The diagram shows relationships that make project management both universally applicable and unique to all project work

Cost Control of Capital Projects
AEW Services, Vancouver, BC, 1983, p7

Figure 7-2: The function-process-time relationship (1983)

7.4   Project management models in the late eighties

With the publication of the Project Management Institute's ("PMI") Project Management Body of Knowledge ("PMBOK") in 1987, there were several attempts to illustrate the nature of project management (Figures 7-3, 7-4, 7-5, 7-6 and 7-7).[7]

The 1987 PMBOK document described Figure 7-3 as follows: [8]

One of the earliest illustrations of project management was developed by the Project Management Institute's Board of Directors

"It is possible to depict the environment of project management and its related body of knowledge in a number of different ways. Venn diagrams [as shown in Chapter 5 Figure 5-1] and three dimensional matrices or boxes [as shown in Figures 7-6 and 7-7] are all feasible."

"Figure 7-3 attempts to show the role of the PMBoK as a vehicle for creation of change between general management and technical management."

"The explanation of the diagram is as follows: The light gray background represents abstract space. Into this space is introduced the top strip which is intended to portray the whole spectrum of knowledge which is required to successfully conduct industry and business. Of course this includes both the public and private sectors. As the diagram shows, this spectrum ranges from the know-how of general management on the left, through project management, to technical management on the right."

"The next series of strips immediately below are intended to elaborate on the top strip. The central overlay circle encompasses the four key constraints of scope, cost, time and quality. As every project manager knows, these restraints are inextricable intertwined. Scope-quality represents performance, scope-cost represents viability, cost-time represents effort, and quality-time represents competitiveness."

The 1987 PMBoK committee felt that the fundamental building blocks of project management were the three basic project management functions of every project. These elements, schedule, cost and technical performance, were presented as a triangle. Interestingly, this "basic" triangle was adopted by Professor H. Kerzner as the motif for the cover jacket of his book "Project Management: A Systems Approach to Planning, Scheduling and Controlling" (Figure 7-4).[9]

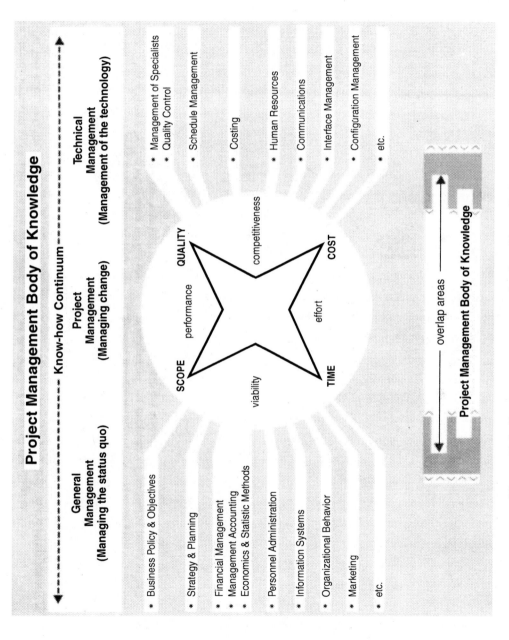

Figure 7-3: Project management body of knowledge setting

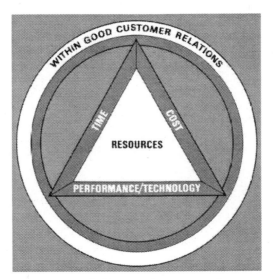

Figure 7-4: Kerzner's cover jacket

Given the fundamental building blocks of Figure 7-4, the PMBoK committee of the day felt that the simplest format was to portray the essential characteristics of every project in three dimensions (Figure 7-5).

Perhaps the easiest model of project management to visualize is a three dimensional matrix

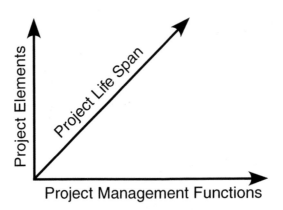

Figure 7-5: A three dimensional matrix

There was little argument about the "Project Life Cycle" but the relationship between the other two was more problematic. This resulted in an enlarged matrix (Figure 7-6) that was considered a more flexible and useful framework on which to build.[10]

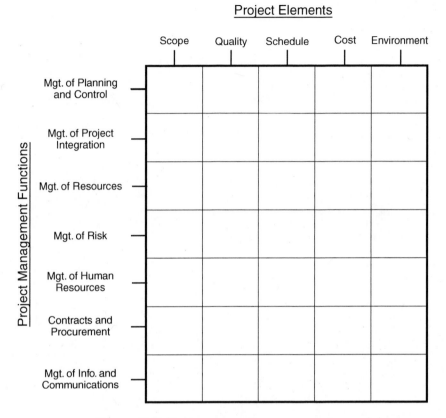

Figure 7-6: Project management matrix model

By 1988, members of PMI's "PMBoK Committee" felt that these illustrations were inadequate given "the difficulties involved in creating a comprehensive yet concise, universal yet specifically applicable document defining the domain of a new profession."[11] Professor Alan Stretton was therefore asked to prepare a critique. To summarize his findings, Stretton came up with a "Three-Dimensional Core PMBoK Framework Model" sometimes referred to as the "Suitcase" (of project management tools and techniques) (Figure 7-7).

The text accompanying the illustration described the model in detail and was further elaborated in Dinsmore's 1993 Handbook of Project Management.[12] Stretton pointed to a number of shortcomings in the original PMBoK and made several recommendations for consistency. However, the Institute appears to have abandoned

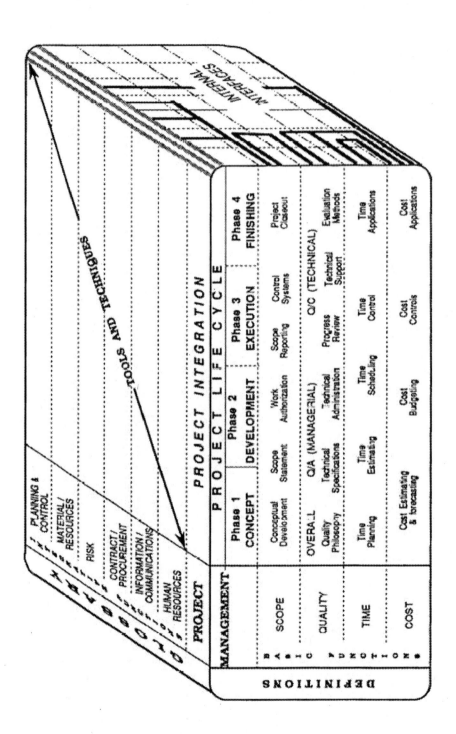

Figure 7-7: Stretton's suitcase of project manager's tools and techniques

this course in favor of producing "A Guide to the Project Management Body of Knowledge".

7.5   Project management models in the nineties

The early nineties saw the introduction of the "Arrow" model as shown in Chapter 3, Figure 3-1.

In late 1991, Warren Allen postulated a more comprehensive three-dimensional model of project management knowledge (Figure 7-8) in a paper titled "The Universe of Project Management: A Comprehensive Project Management Classification Structure (PCMS) to Update and Expand the Dimensions of PMI's PMBOK".[13] The paper arose out of a discussion amongst a group of interested PMI members prior to the annual seminar/symposium.

More attempts to develop models

Allen's model related the nine or more "Level 1" project management functions with the generic project life span and with the potential for considerably extended knowledge in various industry applications. Allen saw the objective as starting "to provide a rational basis for classifying all of the project management information that is a part of our evolving body of knowledge."[14]

The paper provides a good summary of the requirements for such a model and a detailed description of its various elements. It shows how the generic body of project management knowledge is only a small fraction of the total body of knowledge. Unfortunately, PMI subsequently declined the paper for publication, failing to see its prophetic nature, and it appears that the author lost interest.

Meantime, much thought amongst members of the Internal Project Management Association ("IPMA") in Europe was being given to the content of project management. However, great difficulty was encountered in trying to reach any sort of consensus on any relationship structure. Then, around 1996, as a compromise, the "Sun Wheel" consisting of 28 subject areas was published (Figure 7-9).

This author made another serious attempt in a presentation at PMI's 1997 annual seminar/symposium. The paper was entitled "A Project Management Knowledge Structure for the 21st Century" and so addressed not how to do project management, the subject of most papers, but what such a "knowledge structure" should look like, and the need and value of an acceptable model. The work was

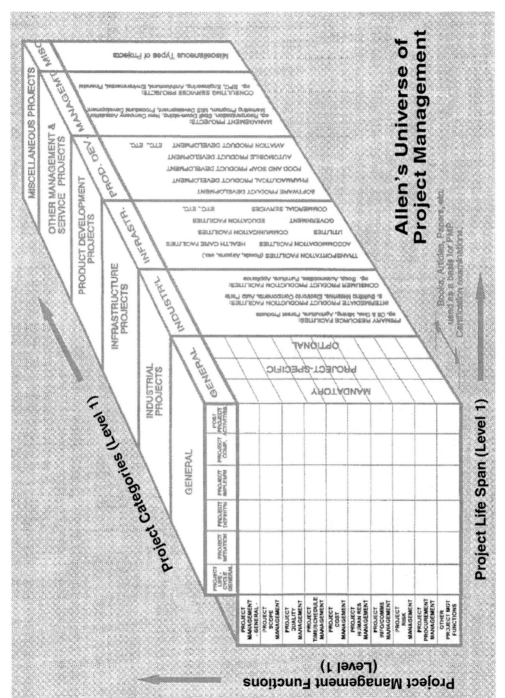

Figure 7-8: Allen's Project Management Classification Structure

based on the idea of "concept mapping" and drew heavily on work by previous authors over the years.

Figure 7-9: IPMA's sun wheel

The paper discussed how to set about such a concept map, the right perspective, the objectives, assumptions necessary, what to include or not, and relevant definitions of terms. However, at the core of the concept map is the idea of a project commitment between a project manager and his/her team and a client/sponsor to produce

At the core of the concept map is the commitment by the project team to deliver the product to the sponsor

some agreed product within prescribed constraints. The resulting concept map is shown in Figure 7-10 complete with object relationships and attributes. The full paper can be seen on my web site.[15]

The 1997 paper was succeeded the following year with another paper in which more detail was suggested together with a concomitant work breakdown structure, a technique more familiar to most project management practitioners. The 1998 paper titled "Defining Project Management Knowledge as a Basis for Global Communication, Learning and Professionalism" can also be seen on my web site.[16]

7.6   Project management models in the new century

Around the same time as the 1997 and 1998 papers were being prepared, Forsberg, Mooz and Cotterham were developing a new and innovative perspective on project management. This work was based on their extensive collective experience with thousands of working project managers and reflected what they considered to be the four essential elements of project management: a common vocabulary, teamwork, the sequential project life cycle, and management elements. The relationship between these elements is shown in Figure 7-11.

An innovative, dynamic "traveling wheel" model

This model is intended to be dynamic and consists of three parts. First, the wheel consisting of nine spokes represents: Project requirements; Organizing options; Project team; Project planning; Opportunity and risk; Project control; Project visibility; Project status; and Corrective action. The rim, Project leadership, holds the whole wheel together. This wheel rotates and progresses along the life span axle.

The axle consists of a series of stages: User; Concept; System; Plan; Sourcing; Implementation; Deployment; Operations; and Deactivation. However, the axle itself also consists of the three aspects (Technical, Business, and Budget) that must be simultaneously managed if the project is to succeed in all three. The whole is supported on the two pillars of: Common vocabulary and Teamwork, held together by Executive support, as shown in the illustration.

The authors describe the model as follows:

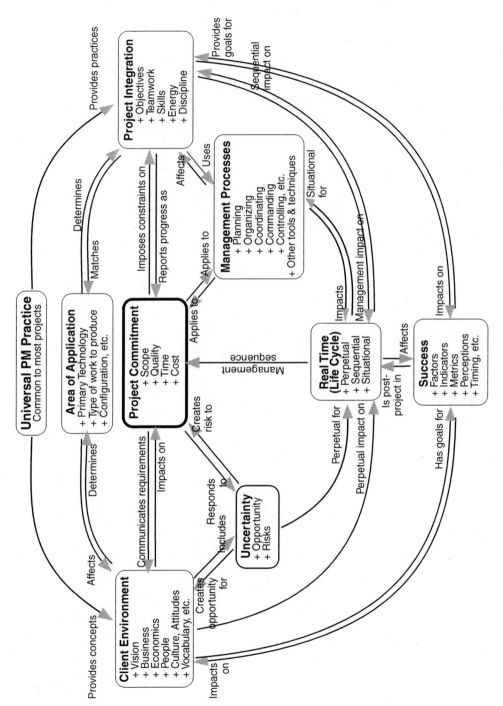

Figure 7-10: Wideman's concept map of project management

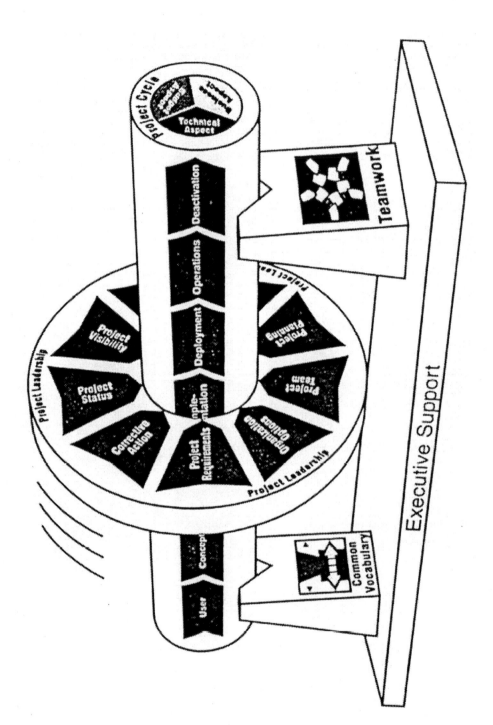

Figure 7-11: Forsberg, Mooz & Cotterham's "orthogonal" model of project management

Crucial to our understanding of project management is the recognition of sequential and situational conditions that require different management responses

"The axle and the wheel represent the overall project management process. Crucial to our project management approach is the recognition of sequential and situational aspects of management as separate domains. The axle represents the gated project cycle and the wheel represents the situational application of the techniques and tools of the ten management elements to manage the project throughout the cycle."

"The relationship among the project cycle phases (the axle) and the management elements (the wheel) is orthogonal and dynamic, as the wheel moves along the axle with progress. The wheel and axle rest on the two piers of vocabulary and teamwork, two perpetual essentials without which the cycle and elements could not function effectively. These four essentials are reinforced by executive support."[17]

Another ongoing initiative is the voluntary efforts of a group of worldwide knowledgeable participants under the leadership of Professor Lynn Crawford, Director of Program, Project Management, University of Technology, Sydney, Australia. This group has met intermittently for the purpose of "identifying and developing a globally agreed body of project management knowledge as the basis for genuinely global and transferable project management standards, certification and accreditation programs … The philosophy is that the work of the group draws credibility from the voluntary participation of recognized opinion leaders in project management, contributing on the basis that all inputs of the group will be in the public domain. This group is working together in the interests of development of project management as a profession and a discipline."[18]

World-wide opinion leaders develop a "Mind Map" of the scope of project management

A slightly simplified version of the resulting "mind map" is shown in Figure 7-12.

By 2002 Microsoft recognized the relationship that quality has with scope, time and cost. In their Microsoft Office Online web site Assistance for Microsoft Project 2000, they illustrate "The Quality Triangle" as shown in Figure 7-13[20] (in essence, reverting back to the simpler triangle of the late 1980s.)

As Microsoft explains:[21]

"Quality, a fourth element, is at the center of the project

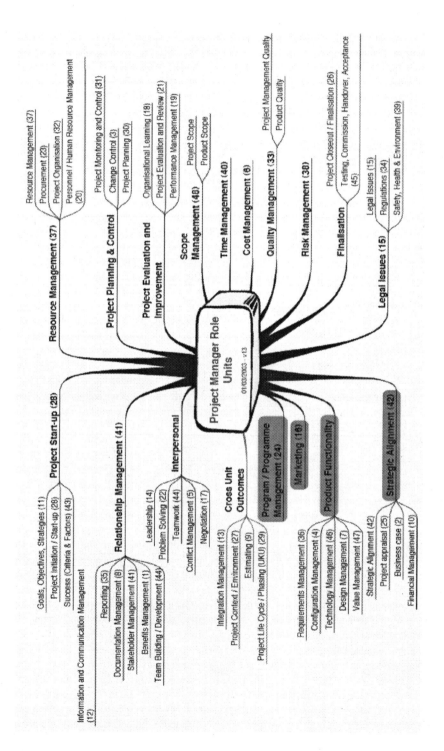

Figure 7-12: Crawford's mapping of "project manager role units" (circa 2003)

(**Note:** For a larger image of Figure 7-12 visit my web site.[19])

triangle. Changes you make to any of the three sides of the triangle are likely to affect quality. Quality is not a side of the triangle; it is a result of what you do with time, money, and scope."

"For example, if you find you have additional time in your schedule, you might be able to increase scope by adding tasks and duration. With this extra time and scope, you can build a higher level of quality into the project and its deliverables."

Lower quality may result from cutting costs. The better alternative is to reduce the scope

"Or, if you need to cut costs to meet your budget, you might have to decrease scope by cutting tasks or reducing task durations. With decreased scope, there might be fewer opportunities to achieve a certain level of quality, so lower quality may result from the need to cut costs."

Money   **Scope**

Quality

Time

Figure 7-13: Microsoft's quality angle

We don't entirely agree with the first statement but it is a step in the right direction. However, Derrick Davis has an even better idea, he proposes the tetrahedron which we have drawn in Figure 7-14. [22]

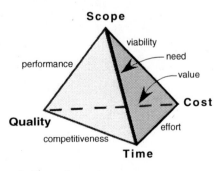

Scope

viability

need

performance

value

Cost

Quality

effort

competitiveness

Time

Figure 7-14: Davis's project management tetrahedron

Note the addition of the ideas of "need" and "value", as represented by the combinations of scope-time and cost-quality.

7.7   Summary

There are plenty of opportunities for further development of project management

If the illustrations we have shown can be accepted as evidence, then project management has clearly come a long way since the 1970s. For example, judging from the mind map in Figure 7-12, the subject is now much more comprehensive. Conceivably it could still be expanded further by such potential additions as stakeholder management, cash flow management, data management, document storage and retrieval management, management of cultural differences, and even vocabulary management as implied in Figure 7-11.

With a little imagination, and research reading, one could add several more, such as critical chain buffer management,[23] customer relations management, issues management, public relations management, and even knowledge management[24] itself – the list seems almost endless. So, how best to depict project management graphically is problematic and depends partly on the purpose of the map and the corresponding illustration.

But are we aiming high enough? If project management is to succeed as pervasively as projects have now become, it must capture the attention and imagination of senior executives. Their perspective is quite different as the grayed areas in Figure 7-12 begin to suggest. We believe that the commitment to delivery between the project management team and the project sponsor, owner or client as suggested in Figure 7-10 is the compelling rationale for project management. And further, that this commitment must be conducted consistent with a robust project life span of control.

In the next chapter we'll introduce a quite different model approach.

References

[1] Senge, P.M., The Fifth Discipline: The Art & Practice of The Learning Organization, NY: Doubleday, NY, 1990, p68
[2] Ibid., p204
[3] Ibid., p400
[4] The Wideman Comparative Glossary of Project Management Terms at http://www.maxwideman.com/pmglossary/index.htm

[5] Original source unknown, possibly a federal government publication circa 1981. Copied from Cost Control of Capital Projects, BC: AEW Services, 1983, p9

[6] Ibid., p7

[7] Project Management Body of Knowledge, PA: Project Management Institute, 1987, pages 1-5, 2-3, 2-4, 2-5

[8] Ibid., pages 1-4, 1-5

[9] Kerzner, H., Project Management: A systems Approach to Planning, Scheduling and Controlling, NY: Van Nostrand Reinhold, 1989, (cover jacket)

[10] Ibid., page 2-5

[11] Editor's Note to A Consolidation of the PMBOK Framework and Functional Components by A. Stretton, Project Management Journal, Vol XX, PA: Project Management Institute, 1989, p5

[12] Stretton, A. M., Developing a Project Management Body of Knowledge, Chapter 3 in The AMA Handbook of Project Management, NY: American Management Association, 1993, p32

[13] Allen, W.E., P.Eng., CMC, PMP, Panalta Management Associates Inc., Calgary, Alberta, 1991

[14] Ibid.

[15] Wideman, R.M., A Project Management Knowledge Structure for the 21st Century at http://www.maxwideman.com/papers/knowledge/intro.htm

[16] Wideman, R.M., Defining Project Management Knowledge as a Basis for Global Communication, Learning and Professionalism at http://www.maxwideman.com/papers/global/intro.htm.

[17] Forsberg, K., H. Mooz & H. Cotterham, Visualizing Project Management: A Model for Business and Technical Success, 2nd Edition, Wiley, NY, 2000, 44.

[18] Crawford, L., briefing notes by Email 5/9/01.

[19] For a larger image of Figure 7-12, go to http://www.maxwideman.com/papers/pm-models/intro.htm and click on Figure 14.

[20] The Quality Angle displayed in Microsoft Office Online > Assistance > Office 2000 > Project 2000 at http://office.microsoft.com/assistance/, 2003.

[21] Ibid.

[22] Davis, D., by Email 12/10/03

[23] Sood, S., Taming Uncertainty, PMnetwork, Project Management Institute, March 2003, p57.

[24] PM Perspectives, PMnetwork, Project Management Institute, May 2003, p2 & 33.

CHAPTER 8

A model with portfolio potential

8.1   A logical progression

*A potential
model for
project
portfolio
selection*

In this chapter we present a speculative model that has the potential for assisting in the difficult issue of project portfolio selection. The objective is to start people thinking and talking about this relatively new area of project management responsibility and the possibility of characterizing projects by unique numbers. The breadth of application may be limited but is certainly relevant to administrative and IS/IT type projects. This work is the result of intensive study by Joe Marasco and myself following on his paper "The Project Pyramid" published April 2004 in the Rational Edge, IBM's software development magazine.[1]

*The model
spans from
project
selection to
realization of
its benefits
that are
normally
beyond
the project
manager's
responsibility*

Of course, project management is a construct that is both complex and controversial so it is unlikely that there will ever be a model that truly represents project management and satisfies everyone. Still, we are hoping that some of these great new ideas will bask in the sunshine of constructive criticism. Note, however, that the concepts are advanced and the material is philosophical, so you have been warned!

The model we shall describe spans the whole of the project management system to relate project resource inputs directly to realization of ultimate product benefits after the project has been completed. The ultimate project benefits are normally beyond the realm of the project manager's responsibility.

In the last chapter we asked why we should model at all and observed, among other things, that models can broaden our perspective and allow people to see a larger picture. This is particularly true when the concepts are abstract. And so it is that Joe Marasco has taken the tetrahedron displayed in Chapter 7, Figure 7-14, and concluded that it is incomplete. As he says in his paper:

> "While I agree with Max's insistence on quality as a critical fourth factor, I believe that his model still leaves something to be desired. When thinking about a project prior to beginning any work on it, management is typically interested in the "shape" of the project – an interest that maps nicely to the four parameters [shown]. That is, we can state *how much* we intend to do (scope); we can describe *how well* we are going to do it (quality); we can describe *how long* we are going to take to complete the project (time); and we can talk about *how much it will cost* to do it (resources). But are we done with our project description?"

As well as scope, quality, time and cost, management is always interested in a fifth variable: i.e. risk

"I don't think so. Management is always interested in a fifth variable: *risk*. That is, given the previous four parameters and the plan that goes with them, management wants to know whether the project represents *high, medium, or low* risk to the business. We know from considerable experience that projects have different risk profiles, and good management tries to balance its project portfolio by having a spectrum of projects with different risks. The more risky ones have a greater probability of failure, but perhaps they have bigger payoffs, too. Just as in a financial investment portfolio, a company diversifies by having many projects with different risk/reward profiles such that, statistically, the enterprise prospers." (Emphasis added)

8.2   Enter the Marasco pyramid model

So Joe proposed a pyramid with the base representing the original four variables and the height representing risk. That is also interesting because "risk" has always been a bit of an outsider in project management circles, neither a project constraint nor one of the facilitative functions in the traditional line up of eight project functional divisions.

Marasco's pyramid model uses the sides and not the corners

But then he said, "let's assign extensive properties *to the sides* instead of the vertices." He also wanted all sides to have compatible metrics for their characteristics, i.e., the measures of all sides must move in the same direction. In other words, more scope is good, more quality is good, more speed (i.e., a faster "pace", the inverse of time spent) is good, and more *frugality* (of resources, i.e., less cost) is good. Next, he tackled the pyramid's altitude. More risk is not good, but more success is, so we have the converse, *probability of success*, as the vertical dimension (Figure 8-1).

To increase the probability of success you must decrease one or more sides of the base to maintain constant volume

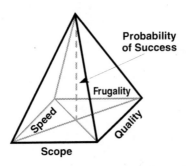

Figure 8-1: Marasco's project pyramid model

Joe then posited that for a given project and its implementation team, the *volume should be a constant* – a sort of project criterion value. That is, the volume is proportional to:

"challenge x probability of success"

The pyramid's base represents the project's "challenge"

As one goes up, the other must go down. For example, if we want to increase the chances of success, then we must *decrease one or more sides of the base* to reduce its area. Another way of looking at it is that maximizing the area of the base also maximizes the profitability of the project by simultaneously maximizing the value of the product and minimizing the cost to produce it. Hence, what we are trading off is profit versus probability of success. Interestingly, this is a fundamental premise with which every project manager is intuitively familiar.

8.3   A problem, and a solution

But then Joe observed a problem with the success scale. Higher is obviously better, but probability never exceeds (or even reaches) 100%, so you cannot double the probability of success by going from 60% to 120%. A different scale is needed that is not in fact far away. We could assume that project outcomes, in Joe's case software development projects, conform to the positive side of the well known "bell-curve" as shown in Figure 8-2. Hopefully, we don't launch any projects with planned negative outcomes!

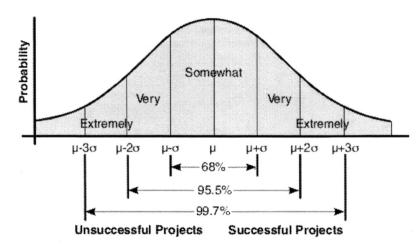

Figure 8-2: Project outcomes related to the standard probability bell curve

Now, for projects whose performance is proportional to the product of many uncertainties, the distribution of successful outcomes can be expressed as a lognormal distribution using the standard deviation (sigma) as the scale of outcomes (Figure 8-3). Note, however, that for projects where performance tends to be proportional to the sum (not product) of many uncertainties, the distribution tends to be normal.

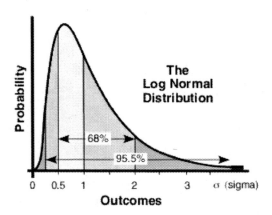

Figure 8-3: Log normal distribution of positive outcomes only

The mid-point of the bell curve (Figure 8-2) is "μ", and in Figure 8-3 it is coincident with 1 sigma. That is, half the area to the left of 1 sigma and half to the right, assuming that our distribution of projects is correct. If that is true, then clearly we want our latest project to fall to the right.

However, the meaning of sigma is different in this distribution in that you accrue area a little differently, i.e., below 1 you halve but above 1 you double. So, as shown in Figure 8-3, 68% of the area lies between 0.5 and 2.0 sigma, and 95.5% lies between 0.25 and 4.0.

8.4   Application to real projects

What are the implications of this distribution for real projects? I'll leave it to Joe to explain:[2]

"Because the peak of the curve lies at around 0.6 sigma, we see that the most likely outcome (as measured by the curve's height) is an unsuccessful project! In fact, if the peak were exactly at 0.5 sigma, your probability of success would be only around 16 percent:

$$50\% - 1/2(68\%) = 50\% - 34\% = 16\%.$$

We should not be surprised by the results we are getting

Since the peak is not at 0.5 sigma but closer to 0.6 sigma or 0.7 sigma, the probability of success is a little higher – around 20 percent."

"Now this is starting to become very interesting, because the Standish CHAOS report, of which I have always been skeptical, documents that around four out of every five software development projects fail. This is a 20 percent success rate ... [So] it is interesting to note that the lognormal distribution predicts the Standish metric as the most *likely* outcome, which may mean that most development projects have a built-in difficulty factor that causes the lognormal distribution to obtain." (Emphasis added)

In short, we should not be surprised at the outcomes we are getting.

8.5   Bottom line . . .

Of course the model makes a number of coarse assumptions and therefore has its limitations with consequent caveats. Not least of these is that in practice you cannot make major changes to any one side without affecting the others. For example, just doubling the resources, a common practice, simply produces congestion at the work face and so does not produce the desired results of halving the time. For Joe's complete commentary, you should read the full paper: *The project pyramid.*[3]

In practice you cannot make major changes to any one side without affecting the others

Nevertheless, the model does make one thing clear. If you want to significantly improve the chances of success of risk-prone projects, fiddling around with a mere 10% or even 20% contingency is not the answer! As Joe says:

> "The simple pyramid model also shows how much you **must** trade off to improve your probability of success. Although it is speculative, the model helps us to soberly decide whether we are willing to invest the resources required to raise our probability of success above the minimum threshold acceptable for our business, given the scope, quality, and time constraints that we specify."[4]

Project plans are typically overly optimistic – by a lot!

The fact is most initial project plans are overly optimistic, either by design or by default. By design because we don't want this project to get killed before it is even started, or because we simply don't know any better – or both! So, project plans are typically overly optimistic by a lot. And, by the time the project manager and other management realize by just how much, it is too late. At that point they will typically try to band-aid the situation with a 10% to 20% patch on only one variable when in fact they need to do much, much more to get to even a fighting chance of success.

So, we should use the concept phase of every project to at least correctly calibrate the remaining big unknowns and the quality of the team. If there is little chance that we can increase the volume of the pyramid at this point, then we **must** re-evaluate the area of the base and focus on the altitude. If we don't do that, then we are simply driving straight through the "orange light" as it flashes before our very eyes at the start of the definition phase. Iterative development especially, cannot work if we do not start adjusting the length of the legs when it becomes apparent that our altitude is far too short.

8.6   The pyramid volume as a key project criterion

Just exactly how the intrinsic volume of the pyramid is made up is a bit of an open question. So let us take another look at the structure of the pyramid.

We have postulated a pyramid as representing a project and assigned certain values to the pyramid's base and altitude. The base of the pyramid is a key element representing the key goals, or constraints of the project, if you will, the project's challenge. This has to be balanced off against the probability of success on the vertical dimension, the whole (i.e., the volume) representing some sort of project "criterion value". Since we are proposing that the sides may be "adjusted" to achieve acceptable levels of risk (the inverse of success), or otherwise to change the criterion value, the question is, what is the real shape of the base and how can it be justified?

Project management is the application of appropriate processes to get from inputs to outputs

A "project" is a "system" in the true sense of Peter Senge's 5th discipline.[5] The system consists of inputs, processes and outputs and the objective of project management is to get all the elements into reasonable balance for a specific outcome. Project management is, of course, the application and management of appropriate processes applied to the system to get from inputs to outputs, i.e., the conversion of raw assets into valuable assets. These processes, by the way are generally referred to as "Tools and Techniques", in the parlance of the Project Management Institute. Figure 8-4 illustrates the simple input-process-output sequence.

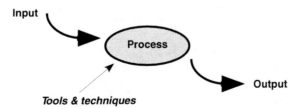

Figure 8-4: The Project Management Institute's view of a project

The benefit value of the specific outcome, the output, is (or should be) measured in terms of value added, i.e., return on investment, but we'll set that aside for the moment. The way we go about a project is that, in the concept phase, we devise a product in the general form of a scope description (however broad to start with) and establish a quality grade. Together these two provide the baseline for our product and these two vectors imply a certain output "asset cost" (Figure 8-5).

Figure 8-5: Relation between scope, quality and cost

The construction, or execution, phase is where the major effort of the project is undertaken

Having established our product description, we then proceed to the definition phase of the project for purposes of establishing a plan and obtaining approval for a construction phase. The construction phase is where the major effort of the project is undertaken. Indeed, for purposes of our simplistic model we can probably ignore the first two phases of concept and definition (as many companies actually do), or at least treat them as overhead on the follow-on phases of execution and transfer.

So, in the definition phase we come up with a plan that essentially proposes the application of appropriate resources over a period of time that will result in the required output, i.e., the required {resources x time} combination. {Resources x time} represents the application or consumption of assets in order to produce a new asset of increased value and these two vectors imply a certain input cost (Figure 8-6).

Figure 8-6: Relation between resources, time and cost

Now when we compare Figure 8-6 with Figure 8-5 we see that we have a common metric for both input and output. If we have developed our plan correctly, the costs in each case should match

– assuming all else is also properly accounted for and matched. Or in other words, we can equate one to the other (Figure 8-7).

Figure 8-7: Matching project inputs to project outputs

That is to say, when we put the two together we have a "fit" (Figure 8-8.)

Figure 8-8: Matching input to output to arrive at Marasco's pyramid base

When viewed in this way, the "$$" line shown reflects the project commitment, the justification and basis for project management, namely:

The commitment given by the project team to deliver the output: upon commitment by the project sponsor to provide the resources!

Several interesting things emerge from this approach:

- We no longer have to speculate on the relationships between the parameters. For example, an increase in scope or quality will drive an increase in resource usage, or time to complete, or both

- We don't have to worry about the shape of the polygon, it is self-positioning – so long as the angles between resources and time, on the one hand, and scope and quality on the other, are at right angles

- The two triangles must "fit" together; otherwise we don't have a viable project. In practice there are always by-products and wastage and these must be factored in as part of the scope

By-products and wastage must be factored in as a part of the project's scope

- If the triangles don't fit we must make appropriate adjustment in any one or more of the variables to have a viable project, still maintaining the right angles of course

With the triangles assembled as shown in Figure 8-8, you can see that we have now established a basis for the shape of the base of our Marasco pyramid. Conceptually, the two triangles match on their diagonals. In practice, there is often the need for intermediate products and always a question of variable productivity and wastage as in any process.

So, although the two triangles match on their diagonals, we still need to take account of the areas of both triangles on either side of the commitment line. Consequently, as we discussed earlier, we also need to cross over to using pace and frugality instead of time and resources for the metrics to be consistent around all four sides.

Given these understandings, we can see that the value of the product goes up as we make the base bigger, better, and get it sooner, while at the same time being the most frugal in producing it. Maximizing value while minimizing cost optimizes the project for profitability. It's perfectly logical that attempting to make our profit larger also makes the project harder and more risky.

8.7   A closer look at the two triangles

The input triangle

Remember that the objective is to represent the volume of the pyramid as some sort of criterion value for the project. In this way we can begin to test the effects of manipulating the variables, i.e., the sides of the model. To do this we must assign numerical values to the sides of our triangles. We could do this by selecting arbitrary scales for each and, so long as we remain consistent across all the projects to be compared in a portfolio, we can assess their relative merits and the results would probably be valid. However, the only common unit that really makes sense is a unit of money, the dollar, since eventually we want to calculate the volume of the model.

On the input side, the important thing, as we noted earlier, is that the product of {(dollars per unit of time) x (time)} yields total resources consumed to effect the transformation, i.e., the project process. These metrics can be determined using traditional project management estimating procedures. However, as every project manager well knows, there must be reasonable balance between the two. We can postulate "unbalance" as either {(low rate) x (longer time)} or {(high rate) x (shorter time)}. Of the two, the former is preferable because so many things get worse when we compress the time scale. In particular, risk increases considerably not least because there is less time to recover from mistakes.

So many things get worse when we compress the time scale

Still, we can't go too far down the path of low-rate-longer-time for fear of jeopardizing our priorities, missing a market window, or simply falling victim to Parkinson's Law.[6] Clearly project management, and especially the management of time, is an art form and our flexibility is relatively limited.

The output triangle, and enter the unit of quality, the "qual"

Scope and quality is a little more difficult to work with because we need a measure for quality. Here, we are not just talking about quality as in "conformance to requirements" but quality as in quality *grade*, or feature sets, if you will. We might adopt a quality unit of "quals", in this case "performance-quals" and "feature-quals".[7]

A new unit of quality – the "qual"?

In the case of performance-quals, it is possible to reduce costs by running roughshod (or slipshod?) over good practices either by using inferior skills or by rushing production. Nevertheless, it has been well established that the penalty costs for non-compliance typically far exceeds the costs of compliance and it does require the necessary up-front investment of both effort and time as we noted earlier. That is why we should always lobby for investment in quality of performance – it just makes good business sense. Figure 8-9 shows the effect of poor project quality on long-term cumulative cash flow, i.e., return on investment.

Weibull and others have observed the "bathtub curve" effect in life span reliability/failure analysis of information technology products and systems.[8] Joe Marasco has shown how this can also be applied to software development projects as illustrated in Figure 8-10.

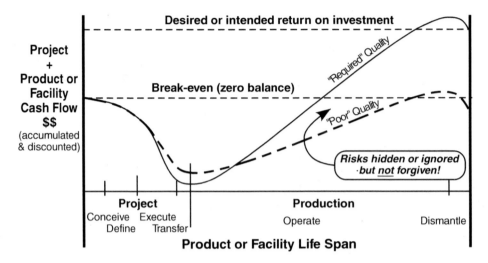

Figure 8-9: Consequent risk of poor project quality

Stage of product life span	Failure rate	Hardware reason	Software reason
1. Early	High	Infant mortality	Early gross bugs
2. Middle	Low	Survivors are good	Stable product under light use
3. Late	High	Old age, fatigue	Statistical appearance of lesser-used or more intensive scenarios

Figure 8-10: The bathtub effect reflected in the life of a product

The implication of the table is that it will take time to improve quality. In particular, many quality organizations barely get out of "stage 1" in their software testing. That is, as soon as the bug rate drops they ship the product. At best, they have reached the early middle stages of the testing process. The bad news is that you can stay at that plateau for a long time because statistically you don't explore the nooks and crannies of the product until you do a lot more testing. In fact, the key ingredient to getting to "stage 3" is just a lot of use over a long period. Getting this level of quality in an initial shipment of a product is generally prohibitively expensive both in dollars and time especially when the cost of testing can be transferred to first-time buyers. They may even be satisfied if they can be assured that problems found will be fixed.

In the case of feature-quals, each "feature-qual" of the end product has a certain cost associated with it. The more feature-quals you want in the product, the more expensive it is to produce – and, of course, the more valuable the end product, providing it is actually used! The converse is that if the feature-quals are prioritized in some way, the burden can be eased by dropping those feature-quals that are least in demand.

Projects that have lots of content poorly implemented and projects that are content-light but carefully implemented are both inferior to projects with adequate content and adequate quality

So, once again there is a balance issue at work here. The best approach is to have a reasonable balance between money spent on features (doing more work) and money spent on quality (doing that work well). Put another way, projects that have lots of content poorly implemented and projects that are content-light but carefully implemented are both inferior to projects with adequate content and adequate quality.

Over all, we take a similar approach in comparing projects in an earned value analysis, or comparing risks in project risk management. In the latter case, we multiply {amount-at-stake x probability} to get a risk criterion value. The resulting dollar numbers have no absolute meaning, only comparative ones. But those results do enable us to make some informed decisions on how to reduce unnecessary exposure.

8.8   The height of the pyramid as a measure of product benefit

We still have the height of the pyramid to consider. Here, I think, we can extend Joe's original concept because, as with the sides of the triangles, we need a metric that is compatible with the base measurements.

The ultimate reason to undertake a project is to derive some benefit, sooner or later. This is a difficult concept for many, especially for those embroiled in the day-to-day battles on the ground, so to speak. However, at the time of deciding whether or not the project should be selected or proceed, such decision should not be taken without an estimate of the expected benefits and the probability of them being realized. Once again, the common measure that makes the most sense is money value.

True, many will argue that many of the benefits of multiple projects cannot be assessed in terms of dollars. In response, I would argue that if that is the case, either the project in question is highly questionable, or simply that insufficient homework has been done to justify the project in the first place. I call it lacking in accountability.

The implied value of the product benefit will be many times that of the pyramid base values

There is a point, however. The implied value of the product benefit scale in dollars will be many times that of the scale of the pyramid base values. Most corporations establish a threshold value for acceptable return on investments (ROI). Therefore, it would seem appropriate to use this ROI number to reduce the scale of the benefit value. But projects also exist in a very uncertain world. In other words, success is never absolutely assured. So we need to factor in Joe's estimate of probability of success.

This all suggests the following formula for the vertical height of our pyramid:

$$\frac{\textbf{(value of product benefit) x (probability of success)}}{\textbf{(threshold ROI)}}$$

We could call this the "success criterion value" for the project. Our complete model is now as shown in Figure 8-11.

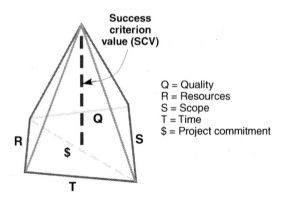

Figure 8-11: Wideman's complete model of project parameters

8.9   The pyramid volume

Remember once again that it is the volume of the pyramid representing the project that we are interested in for comparison purposes. However, there is still an interesting aspect that we have not fully explored. We have discussed the people involved (the resources) and their performance (quality of workmanship) and their opportunity to do quality work (time available and risks involved). However, not all teams are equally skilled, or they may not be suited to the project at hand, or if they are, they may need to go through a learning stage.

The strength of the team must be matched to the technology challenges

Once again, Joe Marasco comes to our rescue. He posits a relationship between the technology challenges inherent in the project and the strength of the team assigned to the task. This relationship is shown in Figure 8-12. Note that the pyramid volume entries in the table are obtained by dividing the team strength by the project difficulty. The "1-2-5" level sequence reflects the general notion that the step up in both capability and difficulty is nonlinear.

Pyramid Volume	Project Difficulty	Green	Competent	Very Experienced
Team Strengths		1	2	5
Few Unknowns	1	1	2	5
Average	2	0.5	1	2.5
Many Unknowns	5	0.2	0.4	1

Figure 8-12: Pyramid volume as a function of team quality and degree of project difficulty

As Joe says:[9]

> "The Golden Rule should be to never undertake a project where the pyramid volume is less than 1. Note that the "dynamic range" of pyramid volumes goes from 0.2 to 5.0 – a factor of 25! This somewhat realistically models what the chances of success will be for equivalent base areas. Project pyramid volumes greatly in excess of say 2 or 2.5 are probably wasteful – due to opportunity cost. But my own experience tells me that anything below the principal diagonal in the above table is cruising for disaster."

> "In iterative [software] development, for example, we need to assess the volume at the beginning of the inception [con-

cept] phase. During inception and elaboration [concept and definition], we get to calibrate the team and reduce the number and gravity of the unknowns. We may start out with a pyramid volume less than one, but my argument is that if it is still less than one when we think we must begin construction [execution], then we should either cancel the project or seriously begin working on reducing the area of the base."

8.10 Summary

As you have seen, we have developed a model that now incorporates the project parameters and the benefits to be derived from the product after the project has been completed. This extends the model beyond the project manager's responsibility to the organization's responsibility. Consequently, we now have a direct link between the project's parameters and the ultimate prize, its benefits.

This should help organizations in two ways:

1. The model provides us with a way of assessing the merits of proposed changes, or the damage resulting from risk events, in terms of the impact on product benefit.

2. If we apply the same metrics to all the projects in a portfolio, we have a way of comparing projects and a starting point for selecting the best possible portfolio.

Is the model applicable to a project portfolio?

Many organizations tend to penalize risky projects more than they should

It has been suggested that the model leaves out any consideration of whether project risks are correlated, which is crucial to understanding portfolio risks. Also, the model leaves out the question of the organization's ability or willingness to accept risk. Many organizations do tend to penalize risky projects far more than they should (and then "bet the company" on one particular project when they shouldn't!)

Further, when a project fails, you not only forgo the benefit it would have achieved had it been successful, but you also lose your investment net of salvage value. Still, sunk cost is not a good basis for determining whether or not a project should continue. An accurate assessment of remaining cost to complete compared to eventual net benefit should be the determinant.

The aim is to relate how much risk is involved to the organization's risk threshold

Certainly the model is too coarse to consider correlation of risk factors. What we are aiming for is an understanding of how much risk is involved, and how that relates to an organization's threshold of acceptable risk. Many organizations will go ahead if they think they have a 50/50 chance of success. Other more conservative organizations won't go forward unless the odds are two to one or better.

We are not suggesting that you try to eliminate risk entirely, that is impossible. What we are trying to do is to get a better understanding of how the other project parameters affect the overall risk profile. In this way executives should be able to make more reasoned decisions, and project managers be able to adjust the parameters when the risk looms too large once the project is in the design stage.

If all of this is true, then we may have just added a new and exciting tool to an organization's project management kit bag.

References

[1] Marasco, J., *The Project Pyramid*, The Rational Edge, IBM, April 2004,
  http://www-106.ibm.com/developerworks/rational/library/4291.html
  (Accessed 8/7/04)

[2] Ibid.

[3] Ibid.

[4] Ibid.

[5] Senge, P. M., *The Fifth Discipline: The Art & Practice of The Learning Organization*, NY: Doubleday, 1990

[6] According to Parkinson's Law, "work expands to fill the time available".

[7] A term suggested by Joe Marasco

[8] See http://www.weibull.com/LifeDataWeb/a_brief_introduction_to_reliability.htm (Accessed 8/7/04)

[9] Marasco, J., by Email, 6/12/04

Part III   *Project Dynamics*

CHAPTER 9

The project environment — Internal

9.1   Who is really in charge?

Since this book is primarily about project management, we'll start from inside the project looking outwards. First there is the project itself. From the selection of definitions presented in Chapter 2, it is clear that projects come in all shapes and sizes and undoubtedly the internal environment of each varies accordingly. This internal environment is generally reflected in answers to the questions: what; where; when; why; who; how; and how much. Managing this environment is where the "soft" part of project management comes in. In other words, this is where we need to invoke such management sciences as psychology, organizational behavior and interpersonal communications, if the project is to be performed successfully!

"Who is really in charge?" is a common question. In fact everyone has a role to play, with their respective authority, responsibility and accountability

A leading question often asked is: "Who is really in charge?" Is it the project manager, project sponsor, owner, financier, the corporate organization and its governing body, or their shareholders and political owners? The list is lengthy and the labels used may also vary with the type of project. Whatever the answer, the important point is to understand that each member on this list has a role in the continuous breakdown of authority, responsibility and accountability.

Typically, the member that needs the change resulting from the project, and therefore who will be its custodian on completion, is the owner. The member that identified the need, and probably its leading protagonist, is the project's sponsor, who may or may not be the same as the owner. If the project is large and/or public, partners other than just the owner or sponsor could finance it. This is usually achieved through some formal financial arrangement independent of the project, though it has an impact on the project's source of funding. In this case, the financier's role is that of holding a watching brief over the project's development and progress in order to protect their financial interests.

If the sponsor is a corporate body, that body is sometimes referred to as the executive authority. Unless the chairman of that executive authority takes personal responsibility, then that body should appoint a ***project director*** as their individual representative. This is to provide singular owner/sponsor direction for the project, through whom proper authority, responsibility and accountability flows down to the project, i.e., to the project manager. Otherwise, failure of the corporate body to do this inevitably leads to fuzzy lines of authority and consequent lack of project control. Unfortunately, failure to fill this position is not unusual resulting in less than satisfactory results, and even compromise to safety on some projects.

Having a project director representing the owner or sponsor of a large project is a good idea

The project manager acts in a service role and so the sponsor or project director is the project manager's client or "boss". It is the project manager's job to take whatever authority, responsibility and accountability is delegated (all three must go together for effective management) and in turn delegate them fully, consistently and completely to appropriate team members for the proper functioning of the project management process. The distribution of this authority and responsibility is usually achieved through some form of work breakdown structure.

Your view of the project will depend on where you are in the project organization

Those under contract to the project may be vendors, contractors, or just simply regular employees. These people fall under the project manager's direction and for them the project manager is their client or "boss". This up/down relationship is continued on down the chain. So your view of the project, and perhaps the terminology you use, depends very much on where you are in the overall scheme of things.

For purposes of this handbook, we will simply refer to the source of the project manager's authority as the "sponsor".

9.2   The project manager's role

It has been suggested that the single common trait to be found among successful project managers is "an obsession with getting things done".[1] However, project managers must have the necessary professional skill and ability to manage their teams and the use of

Proper authority and responsibility brings management status to the project manager

resources through the various project management processes for the project to end up successfully. Still, a significant part of this ability stems from the authority and responsibility vested in the project manager, which brings a certain status and facilitates interpersonal relations enabling him or her to get the project properly organized. It also gives the project manager access to information that enables the project manager to develop strategies for the project team and to make or delegate decisions.

Thus the project manager's role may be amplified as follows:[2]

Interpersonal

As a figurehead, the project manager performs some ceremonial duties on the project. But this is part of the leadership role which ideally should also include hiring and training staff, motivating, counseling, matching staffing needs with project functional requirements, and managing conflict. The influence of the project manager is most clearly seen in this leadership role which also extends beyond project bounds to influence the organization's chain of command and outside contacts.

Informational

Information of good quality is essential for effectively running a successful project

A well-organized project information/communications function will ensure that the project manager receives quality information from subordinates as well as from outside sources and thereby develop a powerful database of relevant information. This database is usually augmented by personal observation as well as by receiving and processing unsolicited information. The project manager thus becomes a nerve center for the project organization and, by disseminating privileged information to peers and subordinates, is able to exercise considerable influence over the project process. The project manager also acts as the spokesperson in conveying information outside the project group and in informing and influencing the decisions of the top management who have organizational control over the project.

Decisional

Information, experience and courage to decide with incomplete data provides the input to decision making. As the project team's decision maker, the project manager may be acting as:

• Interpreter and communicator of project priorities

- Allocator of resources deciding who will get what priorities

- Monitor on the look out for new ideas

- Entrepreneur seeking ways to improve group performance in a changing environment

By exercising these powers, project managers ensure that decisions are interrelated and also retain the power of reviewing and authorizing important decisions before they are implemented.

9.3   Organizational Power Structure[3]

Project managers must have a grasp of organizational leadership, power and influence

The technological and behavioral changes that are shaping the nature of work today necessitate that project managers develop a better grasp of issues relating to organizational leadership, power and influence. With this awareness, they should be able to avoid being overwhelmed by the pathological aspects of modern organizations. That is, the bureaucratic infighting, parochial politics, destructive power struggles and the like, that reduce initiative, innovation, morale and professional excellence.

As examples, an understanding of the Human Resources function will facilitate:

Improving personal effectiveness

Satisfactory direction and progress requires systematic attention to organizational relationships

Project managers typically depend on diverse groups of professional and technical people (support staff and peers) over whom they may have little direct formal control. Therefore, it is imperative that they consider work in more relational terms and recognize organizational power and leadership issues. They need to cut through the web of interdependent relationships and work with a diverse group of staff who, themselves, may be operating under conflicting demands and priorities. Satisfactory progress requires systematic attention to these relationships and to issues of cooperation and resistance as it affects the project.

Developing adequate power base

Project managers need to use their power and influence appropriately to make up for the power gaps that are inherent in their positions. By expanding their personal skills and establishing a powerful information base, as suggested above, they should be able to develop critical cooperative relationships and gain control of important resources. Project managers who are successful in developing such qualities establish a strong track record and emerge as effective leaders in the organization.

Influence and cooperation beyond formal authority

In technical and professional positions there exist power gaps associated with relationships outside of the formal chain of command. This situation is often complicated by other factors that include ambiguity in roles, problems of lateral job relationships, differences in goals, priorities and beliefs of the·project participants, and diversity of locations. Project managers need to identify such factors, assess who among the project participants resists cooperation and why, and design incentives to maximize cooperation *for the overall good of the project.*

9.4   Influencing the project's cultural environment[4]

From the foregoing, the manager of the successful project will recognize the need to spend some effort in influencing the project's cultural environment for the benefit of the project and its stakeholders. Every project team member, indeed every member of the workforce, needs to be persuaded to convey the attitude that "We care!"

Appropriate project management training can improve the cultural environment

Every decision and action should be designed with a view to making the stakeholders' experience better than it would have been had the project not been implemented. Therefore, the project management focus needs to be more on the quality of the stakeholders' experience at every stage of the project than on an overriding preoccupation with computer printouts and weekly progress reports.

From the outset, the project's executive should recognize the important contribution that project management training can make to improve the project's cultural environment. Such training provides a powerful tool in developing competency and commitment to the project, in improving team performance, and ultimately, in final product quality and project success.

9.5   Effective Internal Strategies[5]

Practical experience has identified a number of prerequisites that enable project management success. While these prerequisites do not necessarily guarantee the success of future projects, their absence may well lead to sub-optimal results, if not outright failure. The executive authority responsible therefore has a vital role to play by insisting on the following:

- **Executive support** - the Executive must clearly demonstrate support for the project management concept by active sponsorship and control

- **External authority** - the project manager must be seen as the authoritative agent in dealing with all parties and be the single formal contact with them

Vital internal strategies for effective project management

- **Internal authority** - the project manager must have the necessary managerial authority within his own organization to ensure response to his requirements

- **Commitment authority** - the project manager must have both the responsibility and authority to control the commitment of resources, including funds, within prescribed limits. The results of these decisions must be both accountable and visible

- **Involvement in all major decisions** - no major technical, cost, schedule, or performance decisions should be permitted without the project manager's participation

- **Competence** - the project manager and his supporting team members must be competent. Other functional personnel assigned to the project must also be competent

- **Project team** - the project manager should have a say in the assembly of the project team to assure competence and help in obtaining their personal commitment, support and required quality of service

- **Management information system** - an effective project-oriented information and control system must be in place

9.6   Scope, quality, time and cost: Combinations & relationships

The four core project management functions of scope, quality, time and cost were discussed in Chapter Chapter 3. These objectives or constraints provide the baselines against which the success of the project's management, but not necessarily the success of the product, can be assessed. However, as every project manager knows from experience, these are all very much interrelated and not necessarily mutually compatible. Indeed, many of the project manager's decisions during execution may have to be based on what is an acceptable trade off between the four.

For informed decisions, you must know the project's priorities

It should be noted here that to enable such informed trade off decisions there must be agreement on the priorities among the four objectives. Typically that will be driven by the particular project. Time of completion is obviously paramount for a time-dependent project such as a grand opening sale, when people will be clamoring at the door, even if completion is at the expense of dropping some of the scope. Conversely, projects designed to enhance safety typically require the precedence of scope and quality over cost and schedule. We discuss these concepts in more detail in the next section.

Interestingly, combinations of the four objectives also have significance in terms of the product of the project in the marketplace. This is shown quite dramatically in Figure 9-1.[6]

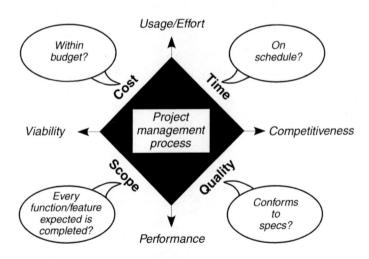

Figure 9-1: The market's view of project management

The combination of scope and cost determine the product viability. The combination of cost and time represents the effort required or the use of resources in the process, while scope and quality together represent technical performance of the product. The combination of time and quality of the product, as well as cost, determines to a large degree whether or not the product is acceptable at a time when it is needed, i.e., whether or not it is competitive.

As we saw in Chapter 7, Figure 7-14, we can assemble the same four parameters as a three-dimensional tetrahedron to add two additional combinations – scope-time representing "need" and cost-quality as "value". Such combinations can also be used as significant measures of project success.

9.7   The tetrad trade off: Varies with type of project

As has been seen earlier, project management seeks to achieve its objectives, as defined by the parameters of scope, quality, time and cost, with the overall perception of the project as being satisfactory, and hence successful. In practice, however, project circumstances often prevail wherein the objectives relative to each constraint may not all be feasible or compatible. This is especially true when considerations of risk and uncertainty come into play.

In most projects, scope, quality, time and cost are not generally mutually compatible

More particularly, as we suggested earlier, some projects may lean more towards one constraint than another. Therefore, the project manager and his team, in the course of managing the project process, must choose options and make decisions according to such priorities. This may be viewed graphically as the tetrad trade off (Figure 9-2).

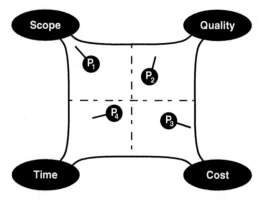

Figure 9-2: The tetrad trade off – emphasis varies with the type of project and often with the project phase

In this diagram, four projects are shown, one in each of the four quadrants of the tetrad. The projects have "handles" which are intended to represent vectors signifying the extent and bias of (or pull on) the particular project as a consequence of the relative influence of the four constraints. Thus, project P1 is in the scope emphasis quadrant and its priority leans towards defining the project scope (rather than developing a defined scope). Good examples include research and development (R & D) and defense projects. Such projects consequently tend to be very uncertain in terms of quality, time and cost.

Priorities among the four constraints typical change during the course of the project

More often the scope is reasonably well defined, but the emphasis is on quality, as represented by P2. Examples include new high-end market automobiles, high-end residential or commercial office construction, or heavy-duty public infrastructure projects where durability and public safety are key concerns. Conversely, P3 is in the time emphasis quadrant, as in the case of meeting the opening day deadline of a national exposition or the opening night of a theater production. Or the emphasis may be on a balance between scope and cost, P4, such as in the case of market research projects or in some government studies.

A further complication is that the priorities among the four may shift during the course of project execution. An example of this would be, say, the development of a shopping mall. At the outset, scope and cost are paramount limitations to make sure the investment is viable in terms of future return. However, as the work progresses to completion, emphasis shifts and cost becomes secondary to time of completion and we see high overtime expenditures to achieve the earliest possible date. This occurs when the daily carrying cost of the project financing exceeds the daily cost of the overtime.

Conversely, a scope and quality oriented project at the outset may well shift towards cost and schedule towards the end of its life span. An illustration of this might be a project that, having experienced cost overruns, is now running out of financing. On the other hand, a cost and schedule oriented project may have a tendency to move towards scope and quality towards its end. An illustration of this might be a product launch which needs to be moved "up-market" as a result of new market competition. Still, such a shift is difficult to achieve in retrospect and emphasizes the importance of sound early project planning and development.

So, managing the tetrad trade off with skill and understanding is an important part of managing a project. Rarely does a project manager have the luxury of a project that has equally balanced constraints such that the achievement of all four is entirely feasible!

9.8   People, information & communications, contracts and risk

The so-called integrative project management functions of human resources, information/communications, contract/procurement and risk have a collective influence on the output of the project. For example, the quality of the project's product will be highly dependent on the skills and quality of the work of the people involved. Although recommended in textbooks on project management, not every project manager has the luxury of choosing the people to work on their project, perhaps the majority do not.

Not everyone is suited to, or comfortable with, project-type work

So you should also be aware that not everyone is suited to project-type work in the first place. You just have to make the best of those available or assigned. Indeed, not every project manager is suited to every phase of the project. You can read more on these particular issues on my web site.[7] Quality of workmanship may also be a function of the quality of the information and instructions people receive. Alternatively, if some of the people are working under contract and the terms of the contract are inappropriate, that could have a harmful effect on the work in spite of effective planning and control.

As we saw in Chapter 3, risk management seems to be some sort of bridging function, perhaps a wild card. When you fully define the project's scope, i.e., its end products, including the quality requirements, then you can estimate and schedule the complete project execution. Unfortunately, in real projects it is rarely possible to define this completely at the outset. Some iteration is usually necessary to offset the level of the project's technological risk. Also, beginning the project with a poor scope definition greatly increases the risk to the project.

9.9   Final comment on the core and facilitating functions

The two types of project management functions that I described in Chapter 3 tend to require different skill sets. The core functions determine the "what", as in "What is to be achieved", and tend to make use of mathematics, as in scheduling or cost control, or mathematical precision, as in specifying, dimensioning, or statistical quality control.

On the other hand, the facilitating functions provide the means for accomplishing these objectives, or the "how", as in "How it is to be achieved". They require positive interaction between people and therefore depend much more on management theory and the social sciences.

Project management is the integration of these two types of management activities, with the ultimate goal of project success, as measured by customer satisfaction.

References

[1] Stretton, A., in discussions 1/17/91

[2] Zuberi, S. by letter 6/5/90

[3] Ibid.

[4] Wideman, R.M., *Managing the Project Environment, Dimensions of Project Management*, H. Reschke and H. Schelle (Eds), Springer-Verlag, Berlin, published in honor of Roland Gutsch, 1990

[5] Ibid.

[6] After W. S. Ruggles & Associates, Inc. training course graphic Section 2, p1, (c) 1989

[7] Wideman, R.M., see series of papers: *Dominant Personality Traits Suited to Running Projects Successfully (And What Type are You?)*
http://www.maxwideman.com/papers/personality/intro.htm,
Optimizing Success by Matching Management Style to Project Type
http://www.maxwideman.com/papers/success/intro.htm
Project Teamwork, Personality Profiles and the Population at Large: Do we have enough of the right kind of people?
http://www.maxwideman.com/papers/profiles/intro.htm

CHAPTER 10

Project controls

10.1   Purpose of controls - to keep on track

From time to time there is a lot of discussion as to whether project management is really an art or a science. Those who specialize in applying the latest tools and techniques to their project work often see it as strictly scientific. For example, management is generally recognized to be the systematic process of planning, organizing, executing, coordinating, monitoring, forecasting and exercising control.[1]

Standard corporate administrative practices are not suited to managing projects

In the project context, control is:

The exercise of corrective action as necessary to yield a required outcome consequent upon monitoring performance.[2]

However, as many practicing project managers have observed, what actually happens on a project seems to be anything but scientific; so there is understandably some confusion. There seems to be even more confusion when it comes to talking about how to exercise control over project activities.

The fact is, the standard corporate management approach of work authorization and record keeping, payment authorization and accrual accounting, and financial reporting on a fiscal basis, is simply not satisfactory for fast-paced highly volatile project work. This is because corporate accounting and control takes an essentially historical perspective, on the assumption that although nothing can be done to change the past, a little tweaking of ongoing activities will improve the future.

In contrast, projects are established for the very purpose of changing the future, a future that can be influenced. So the focus of project management is on future direction. Not just any direction, of course, but specifically towards the predetermined project goals. So, for this special purpose, a different set of controls is required that is specifically project-oriented. In this type of control setup, baseline plans and budgets are established, progress and incurred costs are recorded on a progress-to-date basis, and forecasts are regularly prepared that maintain a constant focus on the end result – in the future.

Project management requires a set of controls that is specifically project-oriented

The project management process might be likened to driving an automobile. First and foremost you must have a sense of direction, a sense of where we want to go. Then you need a road map or a set of directions of how to get there. To get there as soon as possible we select the best route and steer accordingly. What we are doing when we are driving is regularly checking road conditions and direction and making appropriate course corrections. The same mechanism should be true of managing a project. Figure 10-1 illustrates the concept and further suggests that, rather than major course corrections, smoother (optimum) performance can best be achieved by a series of "gentle nudges".

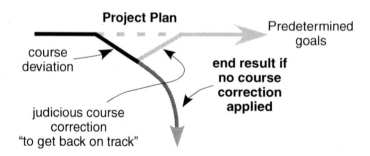

Figure 10-1: Keeping on track

10.2   POETS can be helpful

Perhaps the best way of remembering this equivalent of the quality improvement movement mantra, the plan-do-check-act cycle, is by adopting the mnemonic POETS. POETS stands for "Plan, Organize, Execute, Track and Steer!" (Figure 10-2).

Effective direction requires establishing WHAT is going to be done – and then seeing that it IS done!

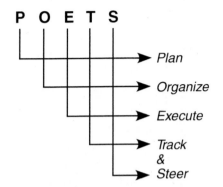

Figure 10-2: Tracking and steering a project

Each component of this ongoing project management process is more particularly described as follows:

- **Plan** - the first step in any project is to plan the project with respect to scope, quality, time and cost. What precisely is to be achieved? Why? What is the process and purpose involved in the end product? How is the job to be done? Why should the project be done one way rather than another? Indeed, why should it be done at all? Where is it to take place? Who will design and implement it? What resources in terms of manpower, materials financing and time are required? What risks are involved? What strategies are required to deal with possible unplanned occurrences? The list goes on.

- **Organize** - the second basic step is an extension of the planning process. A careful analysis must be made of the various activities required in planning and executing a project in order to establish an appropriate project team structure and an inventory of skills that will be needed to complete the project. Then there must be a clear statement of who is responsible and has the authority to execute each activity such as programming, estimating, design, procurement, execution, etc. And, when the time comes, each person must have a very clear idea of the scope and quality that is expected and the time and cost available to complete the activity.

- **Execute** - the methods by which the plan is executed or implemented are critical. No project manager (or other member of the project team) will be successful unless he or she understands the basic needs of human beings, their strengths and weaknesses, mental and social abilities, and how to weld a complex mixture of humans into a dynamic and productive team. Perhaps the single most important characteristic of a successful project manager is his or her ability to manage people.

Without a plan, there is no basis for comparison

- **Track** - continued tracking, reporting and position forecasting must take place during the project, especially during production. The results must be carefully checked against the original plan (or latest plan, if the plan has been formally updated) and any unacceptable deviations faithfully reported.

- **Steer** - unacceptable deviations from the plan should immediately receive management's attention, either by re-allocation of resources or by modifications to the plan (with the Client's approval, of course, if the client's objectives are affected).

From this it is clear that without a plan there is no basis for comparison, no determination of deviation and hence, no satisfactory basis for corrective action or re-direction. Clearly then, what is needed is a system and, in this case, a successful project management system is one which monitors and responds by a controlling action as early as possible after an event.

10.3   Input-process-output and the feedback loop

Whether or not project management is really an art or a science, modern project management does rely heavily on the science of systems to be effective. One of the most basic is the classic input-process-output model with critical feedback loop (Figure 10-3).

Project management control relies on the science of systems

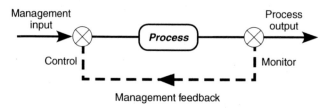

Figure 10-3: Traditional management feedback

Some familiar examples will help in understanding this control mechanism. Consider a simple machine-to-machine system such as an electric furnace or air conditioner. In these machines, the input is the electric power and the output is hot (or cold) air. These devices employ three essential control tools:

1. A monitoring mechanism, in this case a thermostat

2. A comparative device, i.e., the thermostat signal with a set point or objective

3. The means for sending a corrective signal according to a preset formula

The preset formula and corrective signal in its simplest form is on/off. When the temperature range is exceeded, the machine is automatically turned on upon receiving a corrective control signal. It remains on until the temperature is·within range at which point the next corrective signal dutifully turns the equipment off again.

Obviously, other more sophisticated formulae and signals are possible. This can be seen in the automobile example discussed at the beginning of this chapter. In this case, based on the driver's judgment, the steering wheel provides directional control and the gas and brake pedals provide control of the vehicle's speed.

10.4 The Project Control Cycle

By way of contrast, project management is a person-to-person system. In this case, the input consists of requirements, design information, and resources of labor, materials and equipment. The output is the completed product(s) of the project. Along the way, the processing is done by workers with knowledge, skills and experience who transform the raw data through plans to contracts (formal or informal) to execution and finally to completion and transfer of the product into the hands of others.

Project management is a person-to-person system

Control of this process is exercised through tracking, reporting and forecasting the output, comparing this to the project objectives and sending corrective signals to the input of data and resources. Thus, the project is steered towards an output that fully conforms to the project requirements. This management control process is indeed a true cycle because the same cycle is repeated over and over throughout the project life span and is referred to as the project control cycle(Figure 10-4).

The project control cycle diagram shows five elements. Starting with developing or modifying the baseline plan, the cycle proceeds through the logical sequence of monitoring and reporting, analysis of the results, exercising control by modifying critical items, and re-forecasting as an input to the next control cycle update.

Figure 10-4: The project control cycle

10.5 Characteristics of a good control system

In practice, the process of tracking and steering a project is continuous and rather more complex. The cycle described above should continue through all of the project phases right up to the time the project is completed (Figure 10-5). Note however, that the diagram is not meant to imply that feedback necessarily returns to the beginning of the project but rather to the point where the remaining work can still be influenced.

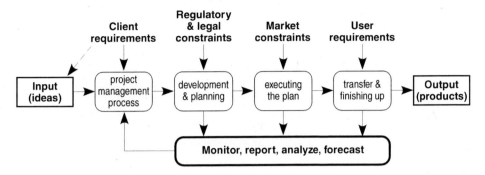

Figure 10-5: Project control in practice

In summary, a good project management control system should:

- Identify objectives and highlight important operations leading to these objectives

- Facilitate detailed planning

- Be able to measure performance in relation to the plan

- Quickly report any deviations from the plan

- Communicate planning and performance information to all parties involved so that appropriate corrective action can be taken

10.6   The "S" Curve as a management control tool

We briefly described the S-curve in Chapter 5 as the progressive cumulative total of the level of effort required (or experienced) during the course of the project life span. Because of the "fractal" nature of project management that we also discussed in Chapter 5, the S-curve effect can be seen at every level in the project life span hierarchy. This phenomenon provides us with a powerful management control technique.

Max's rule of thumb[3]

It is interesting to note that you can arrive at a close approximation to the shape of the project S-curve, within a single phase or activity, simply by plotting two points. Assuming the work or production activity that you are interested in is reasonably coherent you prepare a chart showing 100% time against 100% effort. You then plot two points representing:

One quarter of the work in one third of the time and three quarters of the work in two thirds of the time

Join these by a straight line. Then draw spiral curves on each end of the straight line such that the ends of each spiral are tangential to the straight line and to the horizontal at the start and finish of the chart, i.e., at 0% and at 100%. This plot is shown as curve B, "First Approximation", in Figure 10-6.

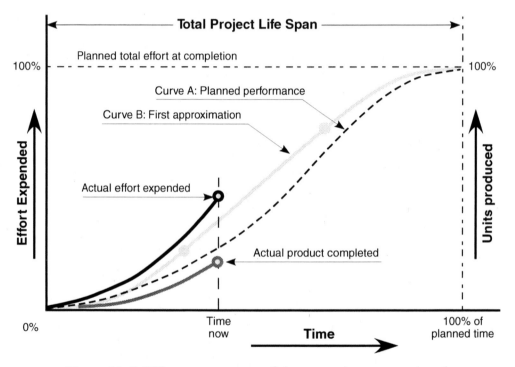

Figure 10-6: "S" curves – a powerful management control tool

I have plotted many S-curve charts on actual projects and found them to be within 10% either way of my first approximation line. The beauty of this rule of thumb is that it tells us the rate of progress you must achieve at peak in the middle third of the span if you are to have any hope of finishing on time. Needless to say, this rate of progress, or pace, is significantly higher than if you simply calculate the average between start and finish. This calculation is most valuable in predetermining resource requirements, including plant and equipment.

To illustrate, a typical curve is shown as curve "A" in Figure 10-6 and, when plotted prior to commencement of the work, represents the planned performance. If, as shown, corresponding scales of effort and units of production are both plotted vertically, it is possible to track concurrently the effort being input and the results being output. Figure 10-6 also shows a situation developing at "time-now" in which both productivity (actual effort expended) and the progress-to-date (actual units completed) are below expectation. This clearly calls for project management action!

As a surrogate you can select a few activities that represent the bulk of the work

The effort expended is typically recorded in direct man-hours or direct costs consumed, but the product is often much more difficult to measure. This is not least because much of the product may still be in process at any given time and require some subjective judgment. Consequently, where feasible, three or four measurable activities, preferably representing the bulk of the work on the project, are selected as major indicators of its health.

The precise shape of the planned performance curve, and particularly its resulting steepest slope representing the period of highest work intensity, will vary depending on the specific elements that comprise its component data. It can be plotted in either percentages or units as a function of time. At the macro project level it can be used to integrate all estimates of labor, equipment, material and overhead into one classic curve. A first approximation to this curve can be arrived by plotting Max's rule of thumb described earlier. This is shown for comparison as Curve B in the figure.

Changes in project scope, conditions in the project environment, or risk events change the shape of the curve, indicating the need for appropriate action if the project team is to stay out of difficulty and meet its project management commitments. As suggested earlier, the results of continuous monitoring presented in this way can send strong signals of problems ahead needing urgent attention. While there are many more sophisticated curves for analyzing various aspects of the work, the S-curve constitutes a basic management control tool.[4]

10.7 Executive Control Points[5]

By combining the concepts of the project life span with that of the project control cycle it is possible to provide a higher level of management control, sometimes referred to as "executive control". In this approach, each phase of the project is treated as a mini-project in its own right, separated from its subsequent phase by an "executive control point". The executive control point is so called because it enables the executive authority having overall control over the project to exercise a go/no-go decision at this point.

Executive control points provide a high level of management control

These points act like closed gates to the project team and are only opened through executive approval. At these points, the project manager must present certain pre-determined "deliverables" to the executive. This enables the executive to make an informed decision on a "go" or "no-go" basis for further work.

> *Approval to proceed should only be granted if the phase deliverables are satisfactory and complete*

The effect is to provide the project's executive with the ability to exercise a high level of control over the shape and timing of the project. In this way, the executive can ensure that either the project is developing in a manner consistent with corporate objectives, or the project can be modified with a minimum of upset and wasted effort.

Costs of changes and delays increase by an order of magnitude in each succeeding project phase

In this connection, it is worth noting that the cost and delay associated with a significant change in the final project deliverables generally increases by "an order of magnitude" in each succeeding phase. Some suggest that this is as high as a factor of ten for each succeeding phase.

These executive control points also provide the opportunity for the executive and project manager to give a boost to the morale of the project team by infusing renewed excitement, enthusiasm and vigor. Equally, these formal approvals provide the project manager with the authority to move the project forward on a renewed mandate and drive it to a successful conclusion of the ensuing phase. It is also an opportunity to ensure that the executive continues to be behind the project and that it is, in fact, proceeding in the right direction.

10.8   The project brief or project charter[6]

Undoubtedly, the most important executive control point in the project life span occurs at the conclusion of the definition phase and before the execution phase. That is because this marks the transition of the project from planning to producing, as we discussed in Chapter 5.

Obviously, this major executive go/no-go decision should be based on sound and well-documented information. Therefore, this information should be presented in a comprehensive document described as the project (execution) charter, project brief or even a "project bible". It should tell the project's executive exactly what they are getting, when, at what cost, and how risky the venture is likely to be.

Thus, this document once approved, becomes the prime source of reference for the project implementation phase. A good project brief or charter on a major project should include:

Not all the items listed here are required in a project charter for a smaller project

- An executive summary
- A general statement of the business aims and objectives associated with the project
- A statement of the project's scope of deliverables (product scope) and quality
- The economic and technological approach to be adopted
- The business justification i.e., the expected benefits of the product, alternatives considered and rejected, and areas of risk of the chosen alternative
- Any regulatory approvals or requirements
- Preliminary design sketches or descriptions, flow diagrams, jurisdictional standards to be met
- The project's master schedule
- The procurement plan, if applicable
- The project estimate and proposed budget appropriation request
- Other resources required from the sponsoring organization (e.g., space, staff, equipment)
- A financial statement and economic projections
- Project cash flow projections
- The project team organization
- Quality, schedule and cost controls to be applied

Obviously the creation of a good project brief requires good project management practices in both the project's planning phases. It will represent a significant amplification of the project's business case prepared by the end of the project's concept phase.

10.9 The function-process-time relationship[7]

This chapter concludes with our attempt to show how the functions of project management, the project control process, and the project phases all relate to one another. These three fundamental components of project management may be viewed as a three-dimensional project system (Figure 10-7).

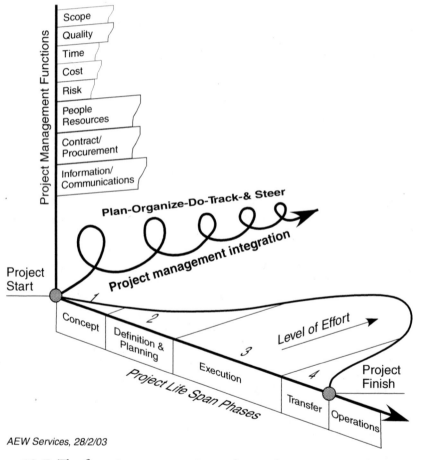

AEW Services, 28/2/03

Figure 10-7: The function-process-time relationship in project management

Each of the project management functions will vary in importance according to the particular project and its environment

In the diagram, the project life span is shown as usual on the X-axis, with its four phases and typical level-of-effort curve with which the phases are generally associated. On the Y-axis are the major project functions to be managed. As we've said, these apply to any project although they may vary in relative importance according to the field of project application or industry. However, the project's management must pay attention to each and every one if they are to get the best out of the project. On the Z-axis is shown the repetitive control cycle which is also of an iterative nature. As time progresses, this control cycle should become more and more focused.

The point of the diagram is that it provides a visual presentation of the project management system. In particular, if the project's goals are to be successfully attained, the project control cycle must be applied to each and every one of the major functions as the project is progressively managed through its life span.

References

[1] *Project Management Body of Knowledge*, PA: Project Management Institute, March 28, 1987, p4-3

[2] Ibid., p4-2

[3] Wideman, R.M., from unpublished text on construction progress monitoring

[4] Kutner, S., *Claims Management, Project Management: A Reference for Professionals*, NY: Marcel Dekker, 1989, p307

[5] Wideman, R.M., *Total Project Management of Complex Projects, Improving Performance with Modern Techniques*, Consultancy Development Centre, New Delhi, India, January 1990

[6] Ibid.

[7] Ibid.

CHAPTER 11

The project environment — External

11.1 What is the project external environment?

*The project
manager
must
take time
to look
beyond
the project*

Obviously, the controlling of activities and events within the project is vital to its eventual success. But equally important, sometimes more so, are the project's linkages to its external environment. The project manager's job is therefore not just confined to internal considerations; he or she must also take the time periodically to look outward.

The project's external environment includes almost everything going on outside the project, so this is a large area to map.

Examples include:

- The technology (the knowledge base it must draw from and/or advances made by competitors)
- The nature of the products
- The customers and competitors
- The geographical setting
- The economic, political and even meteorological climate in which the project takes place
- The environment in which the products must operate
- Other projects competing for resources
and so on.

*Changes in
external factors
can
significantly
affect
the project*

Some of these factors are shown graphically in Figure 11-1. All these factors, and particularly changes in them, can significantly affect the project's progress, its processes and the consequent level of project success.

Generally, the more a project is dependent upon the external environment, the greater the degree of project uncertainty. However, the extent and mix of linkages between the factors will vary from project to project.

It is therefore important to identify the leading factors of concern and their potential for causing problems, assess the probability of their occurrence, and to try to solve them ahead of time, or at least mitigate their impact. Of course, what we are talking about here is the function of risk management.

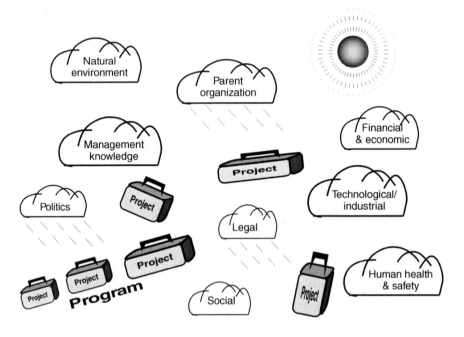

Figure 11-1: The project portfolio environment

11.2   Some typical external influences

The project manager and team must keep aware of external influences that may impact the progress and ultimate success of the project. Some useful examples follow:

- **Sponsor Expectations** - ensuring that the specified project objectives are in fact congruent with the real needs is an important prerequisite during the upstream project planning. Further, it is important that this is monitored for change as cautioned in Chapter 10. This is especially necessary if the sponsor is represented by more than one group with differing perspectives within the sponsor's own organization.

- **Financial/economic conditions** - the viability on which the success of the project was predicated may change during the life of the project and, consequently, require modification of objectives. Examples: increase in interest rates, or fall in economic activity.

- **Technological/industrial conditions** - may impact the progress and effectiveness of the project process. Example: appearance of a competitor's technological breakthrough

- **Parent organization** - the effects of the organization's standards, such as Policies and Procedures, may impact the conduct of the project. Example: revision of corporate policy.

- **Legal and regulatory requirements** - will impact any goods and services contracted for externally "at arm's-length" as well as the conduct of internal activities. Example: stiffening of codes in response to environmental pressures.

- **Political implications** - may be indirect and more obscure but can have a major impact, especially on infrastructure-type projects. Example: change of government at any level.

- **Health and safety standards** - must be observed and, if well maintained, can have a very favorable effect on project morale, progress and quality. Example: the results of workforce training.

- **Natural environment protection** - recognition that natural resources are finite and must be protected and conserved is an important consideration in the ultimate acceptability of infrastructure type projects. Example: other concurrent projects may together overload the natural environment.

- **Changing workforce**[1] - the workforce mix in terms of women, minorities and immigrants is changing in many parts of the world. It is becoming better educated and versed in today's technologies and is moving from manual and clerical to knowledge skills. Example: changes in the perception of acceptable working conditions.

- **Social responsibilities**[2] - includes recognition of shifting needs such as reducing risk, providing interesting work, a healthier environment and improved opportunities. Example: shifting

Any of these external factors could change and affect the project and its ultimate success. So be prepared!

perceptions may result in loss of stakeholder interest in the project.

- **Ethical issues**[3] - hidden information and agenda are no longer acceptable to today's information-conscious public. Honesty and integrity are therefore of prime importance to the success of a project and to an ability to stand the scrutiny of both peers and society once the project is completed. Example: exposure of unacceptable practices on other similar projects may heighten awareness of these issues.

- **Project management knowledge** - is expanding like any other discipline, and project managers have a duty to remain current in both the art and science. Example: better understanding of the mechanics of each of the project management functions.

11.3   The environment from the project perspective

Since the project environment described above is all encompassing, and theoretically extends beyond the horizon, ways and means are necessary for visualizing specific elements. The impact of the environment on a project is shown simplistically in Figure 11-2, and some suggested environmental groupings are shown in Figure 11-3.[4]

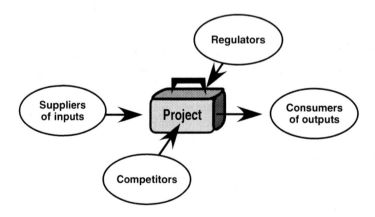

Figure 11-2: The project environment as a process

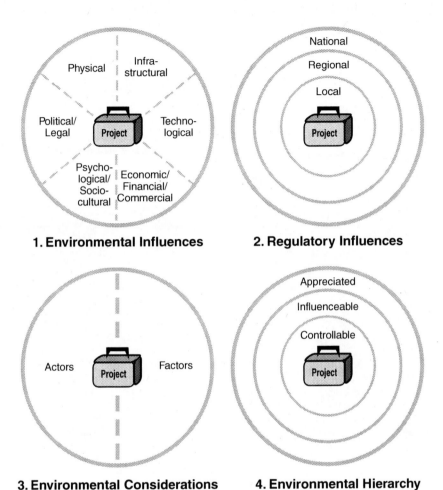

1. Environmental Influences   **2. Regulatory Influences**

3. Environmental Considerations   **4. Environmental Hierarchy**

Note: Influence boundaries are naturally fuzzy

Figure 11-3: Environmental influences on the project

11.4   Developing effective external strategies[5]

Just as the means of influencing the project's internal cultural environment, as described in Chapter 9, was one of developing the right attitude, so it is with developing a sound external stakeholder environment. Perhaps you can best reflect this attitude by adopting a mindset that reverses the traditional organization chart hierarchy. In other words, place the project stakeholders at the top of the chart, followed by the front-line project team members, and on down to the project manager at the bottom (Figure 11-4). Perhaps the project team will then better visualize their truly service orientation, designed to serve the best interests of a successful project outcome, both perceived and in reality.

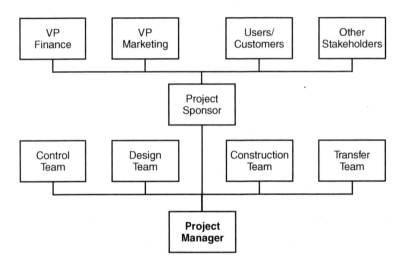

Figure 11-4: Concept of an inverted organization chart

The inverted organization chart illustrates the concept of a project manager as a servant-leader

At the same time, the project manager will also better understand his or her role not just as project leader but also as servant of the project stakeholders. Barbara White has written an interesting paper on the topic of "Can a Project Manager be a Servant Leader? A Reflective Critique".[6] Barbara looks at the definitions, characteristics and responsibilities of a leader, manager, project manager, servant and a servant leader. She draws some interesting conclusions about the true role of a project manager.

Steps in the process:

1. Learn how to identify and understand the role of the various stakeholders, how this information may be used as an opportunity to improve both the perception and reception of the project, as well as in developing the project scope definition

2. Identify the real nature of each stakeholder group's business and their consequent interest in the project

3. Understand their behavior and motivation

4. Assess how they may react to various approaches

5. Pin-point the characteristics of the stakeholders' environment and develop appropriate responses to facilitate a good relationship

6. Learn project management's role in responding to stakeholders' motives

7. Determine the key areas which will have the most impact on the successful reception of the project

8. Develop a Project Acceptance Plan aimed at managing/meeting external stakeholders' interests

Even a minor stakeholder can find a "fatal flaw" in the project – and bring it to a standstill!

Remember always that even a minor stakeholder group may discover a "fatal flaw" in the project plan and bring the project to a standstill!

11.5 Identifying and classifying the stakeholders

One technique for dealing effectively with the project's external environment is to prioritize the various stakeholder linkages by conducting a stakeholder analysis. Such an analysis would be designed first to identify all the potential stakeholders who might have an impact on the project, and then to determine their relative ability to influence it.

Stakeholders may be found in any of the following groupings:

It is useful to identify stakeholder groupings and classify their interests and influence

- Those who are directly related to the project, for example, suppliers of inputs, consumers of outputs, and all those involved in the project process itself

- Those who have influence over the physical, infrastructural, technological, commercial/financial/socio-economic, or political/legal conditions

- Those who have a hierarchical relationship to the project such as government authorities at local, regional and national levels, and

- Those individuals, groups and associations, who have vested interests, sometimes quite unrelated to the project, but who see it as an opportunity to pursue their own ends, such as competitors and special interest groups

Having identified the various stakeholders, each may be assigned to a category according to their relative ability to influence the project. Three possible categories include:

- Those whose requirements can be moderated or constrained
- Those whose requirements can be influenced, and
- Those who need to be appreciated

Within each of these categories, the stakeholders may be further rated by degree of significance according to their ability to influence the project outcome. Appropriate members of the project team can then prioritize their efforts accordingly to maintain healthy linkages designed to provide the greatest probability of ultimate project success.

11.6   Some examples of stakeholders

Primary stakeholders:

- The project workforce
- The project's product users
- The local community
- The community at large
- Special interest groups
- Elected representatives and government administrators, and
- The news media

Secondary stakeholders or participants*:

- Business and professional groups
- Business media
- Labor groups
- Educators and school groups
- Taxpayers, and
- The industrial sector of the project

   * Sometimes referred to as "constituents"

Come to think of it, that seems to cover just about everybody, so it becomes important to classify these people as suggested in the previous section.

11.7   Exercising influence through project public relations

Traditional management has long since recognized the classic input-process-output model with its management feedback loop

Opening communication channels in all directions is a powerful motivator for project participants

for process control, as discussed in Chapter 10, Project Controls. Dynamic managers also recognize that opening communication channels in both directions constitutes a powerful motivator at the operative level. Whether quality information is presented in verbal, written or graphical form, improvement in performance can be quite remarkable. Indeed, many knowledge-workers demand it.

This principle is just as true in the field of projects, though regretfully somewhat less evident. Nevertheless, on a major project, especially if it is publicly funded, providing a general information center is quite common. Even more pro-active, if the project is sufficiently large or important, the interface with much of the external environment may be assigned to a specific group within the project team. This group may be labeled public relations (PR) or some similar title. Their goal is to provide positive feed forward, as suggested in Figure 11-4, and this becomes a vital part of improving the public's understanding and perception, and hence their reception, of project activities and the outcome.

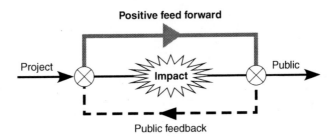

Figure 11-5: Managing the environment – the public relations concept

To a surprising extent, the project team's ability to exercise this positive feed forward will determine their ability to control the project in terms of its schedule and final cost.

11.8 Summary of a public relations program

The strategies discussed above may be briefly summarized in the following sequence:

- Recognize the need to interface with the project's publics (both internal and external)
- Establish a positive "PR" philosophy
- Identify the target audiences

- Develop a "Model PR Program" designed to improve the project's environments
- Develop a work breakdown structure for the PR program
- Implement and monitor the plan
- Run it like a subproject, and
- Enjoy a successful master project!

References

[1] Zuberi, S., by letter 6/5/90
[2] Ibid.
[3] Ibid.
[4] Youker, R., *Analyzing the Project Environment.* 13th Asian Development Bank Seminar MS, Manila, Philippines, 1987
[5] Wideman, R.M., *Dimensions of Project Management* in *Managing the Project Environment*, Springer-Verlag, New York, 1990
[6] White, B.A., *Can A Project Manager be a Servant Leader? A Reflective Critique*, at http://www.maxwideman.com/guests/servant/intro.htm

Part IV *Program and Portfolio Management*

CHAPTER **12**

The program management office

12.1 What can a program management office do?

A program management office is a broad concept with a variety of roles

A program management office is a group within an organization responsible for supply, support, and internal consulting to ensure that projects within its responsibility are carried out consistently and successfully in accordance with company strategies. It can have a range of different responsibilities and report to different levels of the corporate organization. Indeed, in a large organization, there may even be more than one such office at different levels and with different scopes and responsibilities.

The program management office may be known by a variety of different names such as project support office, program office, portfolio management office, or even "War Room" or "Skunk Works". As we saw in Chapter 2 there is a difference between project, program and portfolio management so the different labels for the offices will likely represent different *scopes* of responsibilities. Still, whichever name is adopted, it should properly reflect its *level* of responsibilities – the higher the better. For convenience in this chapter, we'll stay with the name program management office (PMO).

There are a number of things that a PMO can do but perhaps the most important is to establish the organization's project "business model" to:

- Clearly relate projects to business objectives

- Ensure a degree of corporate consistency

- Provide a basis for comparing, prioritizing and tracking different types of project across the whole organization

- Establish a "home" for project managers and project management specialists especially so that they may provide mutual support and benefit from each others experiences and so have their talent and availability used more effectively

- Demonstrate the value of project management to the enterprise

A PMO can also research and implement project management good practices to:

There are plenty of things that a PMO can do without interfering with the project manager's responsibility to run the project

- Remain competitive
- Advance the organization's project management knowledge
- Facilitate and promulgate the best of lessons learned
- Create a mature and professional project management process

As well as:

- Ensure support and informed consent from senior management
- Establish legitimate project management authority within the organization
- Provide support to multiple projects where each project is vital to the organization's well being
- Ensure that all available resources are used in the most effective manner

Another area is to provide customer focus

- Provide a central customer-focused response center for client concerns
- Maintain a skills inventory
- Recruit staff and recommend team candidates
- Assess capabilities and recommend compensation
- Establish policies and procedures to ensure a reasonable degree of consistency of method, application and documentation across the organization, and
- Achieve more consistently successful outcomes

12.2 Program management office services

Some of the opportunities for a PMO include mentoring, training and services. Therefore, senior staff should have perhaps ten or more years of practical project experience and have demonstrated effective "people" skills. The technical staff should have at least five years experience and be competent in each of the project management functions served such as scope, quality, time, cost, change controls, resource allocation, and so on.

Mentoring

- Mentoring to senior management on project selection
- Project management policy direction
- Organizing and structuring complex projects especially the phasing of "risky" projects
- Facilitate, mediate or adjudicate resource and other conflicts between projects
- Or even between clients!
- Providing a second opinion including searching for alternative solutions

Training

- Provision of training for continuous improvement that are responsive to current needs particularly for new staff
- Bridging the gap between theory and practice
- Project scope definition including capturing "customer requirements" and description writing
- Scope development (WBS)
- Project start-up
- Project planning
- Project execution, especially in establishing baseline controls
- Close-out and transfer of the product to the "care, custody and control" of the customer

Services

Some examples of services include:

- Proposal preparation
- Selection of outside consultants, vendors, trainers and courses
- Pre- and post-project audits and reviews, especially on projects that succeed rather than ones that failed!
- Assisting project to recover
- Helping team members generally, especially those who may lack experience

12.3 What are the merits of a program management office?

The benefits to the organization of a PMO include objectives to:

- Ensure project priorities are maintained consistent with business objectives

- Ensure correspondence of project goals to business objectives
- Recognize the importance of project management across the organization
- Make the cultural shift to project management
- Ensure project visibility

Instituting an effective PMO will reflect senior management's commitment to project management

- Provide a career ladder for project managers
- Establish project management professionalism
- Ensure appropriate use of project management tools and techniques
- Facilitate productivity improvement
- Improve project effectiveness
- Act as a repository for past project records, lessons learned and archiving. This reporting will generally serve as the organization's "corporate memory" and hence improve profitability

Further, the disadvantages of *not* having a PMO include:

- Project managers assigned from functional departments may find themselves trying to serve two masters, their department head and the project. This dual allegiance can lead to conflict or an understandable functional bias. Consequently,

- The project manager's effectiveness across functional boundaries is less effective

- Project management skills may be weak or at least not as good as they should be

- Project leaders may focus more on solving the technical aspects of the project rather than managing it

Lack of a program management office in an organization with many projects may reflect a lack of true commitment to project management!

12.4   Program management office policies and procedures

Does a PMO need policies and procedures manuals? Yes, and that can be a major exercise, but it doesn't have to be. Such manuals can be anything from just a set of high-level principles to a set of guidelines to a comprehensive manual complete with procedural details. Whichever approach is adopted, they are needed to establish sufficient uniformity of management that the projects can be managed together as a program or a portfolio. Each policy should have its own standard template to encourage uniform documentation.

Recommendations for policies and procedures are available on my web site.[1] However, a few high-level principles worthy of particular mention include:

The PMO should establish certain high-level principles for the management of all projects

- All projects will be supported by a justification statement and listing of the key success indicators

- All projects must be supported by an approved scope description

- High-quality workmanship is expected on all project work

- No project work will start without an authorization, a schedule target and budget allocation

- Project cost accounting will be based on a work breakdown structure, standardized at a high level

- All projects will be subject to a risk management review that is appropriate to the size and complexity of the project

- No project may proceed without someone formally assigned to lead it with clear reporting lines detailing authority, responsibility, accountability and risk ownership

- All projects will provide periodic resource requirement reports

- All contracted supplies and services will be subject to corporate policies and procedures

- All instructions will be dated, titled and signed by the issuer

12.5   A summary of the pros and cons of a PMO

Arguments for

A PMO can provide an environment that:
- Establishes strategies for alignment with corporate business goals
- Enables economies of scale
- Controls priorities of both projects and resources
- Establishes common control and reporting procedures
- Ensures consistency of approach
- Establishes ownership and accountability
- Establishes auditing criteria

- Tracks quality of work and product
- Reduces risk of failure
- Establishes greater consistency of outcomes
- Promotes repeatability and reusability
- Facilitates review and maintenance of standards
- Represents a platform for improvement
- Ensures consistent training
- Enables learning from experience
- Links to best practices
- Maintains a project management knowledge base
- Is a home for project managers

Arguments against

A PMO is not justified because it:

A PMO must be well-designed to make sure it does not fall victim to the arguments against it

- Has shown no hard evidence to prove that it improves project success rates
- Increases overhead
- Diverts good project staff from managing projects themselves
- Concentrates power in one part of the organization
- Becomes a source of bureaucracy
- Can be process driven rather than product driven
- May exacerbate problems if responses are not timely
- Diffuses project managers' responsibility
- Hinders project manager initiatives
- Inhibits project managers' ability to direct activities
- Creates resentment among project managers
- Stimulates power struggles within the organization
- Causes distractions from the real issue of product delivery

The insightful reader will observe that the pros outnumber the cons by 18 to 13. Not only that, but most of the arguments against a PMO are really arguments against a poorly designed or implemented PMO!

References

[1] For recommendations on policies and procedures see the site map at http://www.maxwideman.com/sitemap.htm.

CHAPTER 13

Portfolio management

13.1   What is portfolio management?

The purpose of project portfolio management is to meet some business need

A project portfolio, sometimes described as enterprise project management, is a collection of projects similar to an investment portfolio. The projects are usually relatively independent, some new, some upgrades or some replacement projects. The purpose of grouping into a "portfolio" is to meet some business need such as overall management and risk assessment. Typically, they share either physical or financial resources (such as the available capital for investment in assets). Consequently, they must be coordinated accordingly to improve collective corporate project performance.

So, the grouping of projects is not because of a specific corporate strategy or initiative or because they have a common theme or work content, that would be a program. Instead, they are grouped together into a portfolio because they come under one organizational unit at a higher level in the organization. That might be a corporate division, vice president level or at least the level of a senior manager.

Screening of projects for a portfolio should be formal, consistent and based on value to the business

Projects that are to be included in the portfolio are identified in the corporate planning process. They should be subjected to a screening or selection process that is formal and consistent. Selection should be based on the value that they add to the corporate business objectives, that is, their "return" on investment. However, the return may not necessarily be in dollar terms; some projects may contribute to corporate goals in ways that are not properly reflected strictly in dollar terms.

This does make comparison difficult and final selection may end up as a subjective decision. However that may be, every project should be based on a viable business case or preliminary feasibility study that is aligned to corporate goals and objectives. That is, all projects in the portfolio should be justifiable in terms of "strategic fit". Having become part of the portfolio, each project should be prioritized and managed from idea to product delivery and beyond.

13.2 What CEOs need to know

When it comes to assessing the value of each potential project, especially for purposes of project selection in a portfolio, what CEOs need to know, as well as those directly responsible, is:

Specific answers are needed by CEOs and portfolio managers

- How much benefit will I get out of this proposed thing?
- When will I get the benefit and not just delivery of the project's deliverable?
- How much will the benefit cost, including production, marketing, ramp up and servicing?
- How risky is this whole undertaking?
- If the project is delayed, what then will be the consequences?

From a project portfolio management perspective what corporate management needs to know is:

- Where are corporate resources being consumed?
- What performance results are being obtained?
- Are project objectives still in alignment?

Or, if not

- Have the corporate goals or objectives changed?
- Have the corporate vision and priorities changed?

Tracking must follow through the product life span, not just the project life span

To answer these questions, you must take a corporate worldview. Tracking must continue not only through the *project* life span but also through the *product* life span to ensure that the intended benefits are realized. This latter [what?] is usually beyond the mandate of the project manager so it falls upon the leader of the project portfolio team. Just as good project management relies on reliable feedback on project progress and forecasting, so too must there be reliable feedback to the portfolio manager on the extent to which actual benefits are in fact realized. Without this feedback, there is no accountability.

13.3 Corporate management requirements and hurdles

So, effective project portfolio management requires:

- A corporate strategic planning process consistently applied across the organization

Project portfolio management requires a high level of management understanding

- A consistent project management process that produces consistent progress reporting especially in the consumption of resource assets
- Standard metrics applied uniformly across the portfolio
- A high level of management understanding in the management of portfolios, so as to allocate resources with competence and sympathy for the inevitable effects of prioritization

Clearly there are some potential hurdles for senior management. For example:

- Do they understand project management?
- Is the feedback information current, accurate and reliable?
- Do project managers accept this level of control when resources are throttled back or corporate priorities change?
- Is the regulatory environment monitored and factored into the decision process?
- Is the necessary information being fed down the line effectively, and is it being acted upon?

The challenge is to determine how many projects the organization can handle within its capacity

Typical problems experienced in project portfolio management include:

- Projects may finish on time and within budget but do not necessarily meet the corporate objectives
- Many organizations initiate more projects than the organization can handle leading to much frustration and disappointment

Almost all organizations are constrained by limited resources. The challenge is to determine just how many projects the organization can handle:

- Of what size and complexity?
- Consuming what critical (i.e., limited) corporate resources?

and making these limits clear at all management levels.

What may be needed is a high-ranking committee appointed to

Appoint a high-ranking committee to determine selection

obtain the data, determine selection and provide direction. This committee could be called an "advisory committee" or "control board", or some similar name and be composed of vice presidents, directors or senior managers. The responsibility for managing the portfolio might then be assigned to a portfolio management office, program or project office such as we discussed in the previous chapter.

13.4   How do you get started with project portfolio management?

The first step is to ensure that there is a corporate strategy, one that can be interpreted for purposes of managing a portfolio of projects. So:

- The corporate mission must be expressed in terms of business direction
- The business direction must be expressed in terms of a working strategy
- The strategy must be translated into specific objectives, and
- The specific objectives must be achieved by appropriate projects

Creating benefit or value is a better goal than "best strategic fit"

You will see from this hierarchy that project objectives should not be set in isolation.

From among the projects, a selection must be made, often prioritized on a so-called "best strategic fit". This assumes that all projects in the portfolio are of a similar scale. However, creating benefit or value, or most value for the investment, is probably a better goal. Then metrics must be established such that each project can be monitored, not just against traditional project management objectives, but also on the continued existence of benefit to be realized from the product.

In setting business objectives, a valuable approach is to adopt the SMART approach. That is make the objectives:

- **S**imple
- **M**easurable
- **A**ttainable/Achievable
- **R**ealistic and relevant, and
- **T**ime-bound

Hence, ask these questions:

- What business are we in?
- What do we want to achieve - and why?
- How will this be achieved?

13.5   Organizational strategy

Structure the organization covering the project portfolio so that it is in sync with the project portfolio strategy. Further, resources and capabilities must also match and be managed with flexibility to meet changing conditions. And, of course, continuously measure *portfolio* outcomes, i.e., the realization of project benefits. Where the results are not satisfactory you must modify strategy, goals and objectives to suit.

If you are just introducing portfolio management you may be surprised by how many projects you actually have!

For those organizations that have projects already ongoing but are switching to portfolio management:

- Find out how many projects there are and who is running them. The answer could be a surprise!

- Make sure the ongoing projects are either mandatory, or ranked as suggested in the next section

Then establish which projects:

- Do not fit
- Are overloading the key resources
- Involve unacceptable risk

Based on this information, prune the portfolio accordingly, but do it prudently!

Managing an organization's portfolio of projects requires sound policies and procedures at the executive level, ones that reflect the corporate strategy. It also helps to know which projects support the organization's highest leverage. In any case, for sound decision-making there must be an effective high-level reporting structure and capability.

Sound and consistent portfolio management reporting requires dedicated enterprise software to be in place. This software must:

- Include a common database covering proposed and ongoing projects

- Enable integration and consolidation of data

- Permit universal access and evaluation, and
- Shift the focus from individual project objectives to higher level business operational objectives

13.6   The project selection process

The sponsoring organization or department typically identifies projects in a portfolio during the annual corporate planning process. Ideas are sought from business unit managers at the start of each corporate planning cycle and presented in some standard format. This format might be an elemental business case or a simple project concept document. Note that project management service organizations, i.e., portfolio management to program management offices, respond to project needs and rarely initiate project propositions themselves.

Every project in the portfolio should be managed from idea through product delivery to delivery of benefits

As we've said, to ensure the benefits of project portfolio management, each project should be managed from idea through product delivery to delivery of product benefits. The potential projects for inclusion in a portfolio should be:

- Subjected to a screening or selection process that is formal and consistent
- Based on a viable business case or specific criteria, e.g., a simple risk assessment
- Consistent with corporate goals and objectives

The only exception, of course, is the case of a "pet project" of a corporate executive! The concept of screening is shown in Figure 13–1.

Project selection is usually the responsibility of a group of senior managers representing the various corporate functional departments. These representatives form a selection committee or corporate steering committee that has responsibility for ensuring that the corporate vision and objectives are implemented.

The committee should place each project into one of the following categories and rank each group based on highest corporate return:

- A government regulatory requirement
- A need to satisfy public safety concerns
- An operational efficiency improvement

- Environmental improvement or public relations opportunity
- New business or economic opportunity

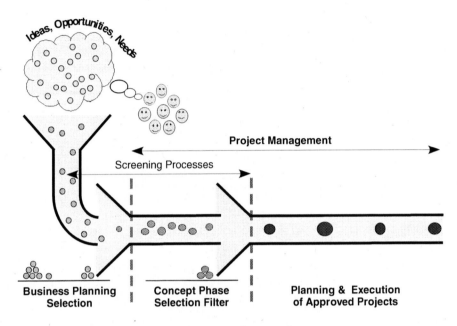

Figure 13-1: Project selection by screening

Selection criteria may include:

- "First cut" categorizing as described above
- Strategic fit, value and balance amongst projects
- Some variation of numerical scoring based on a checklist and relative weighting, or
- Some other decision model

The selection criteria may also include comparative criteria such as:

- Financial analysis including return on investment or internal rate of return
- Cost/benefit analysis
- Economic analysis
- Cash flow or pay-back analysis
- Financial sensitivity to risk, or
- Some measure of benefit other than financial such as contribution to corporate image

13.7   Project selection ranking

You may well find that after going through the selection process there are still more projects than can be funded or resourced during the planning period (typically one year). Assuming you have taken care of the mandatory projects, safety, equipment replacement and so on, the question is "How do you choose the rest fairly and consistently?" Here is a suggested approach offered as a simple example, but you must customize it to suit your own situation. This approach assumes a two-dimension primary ranking and a supplementary list of secondary criteria.

Primary ranking by numbers

After you've identified the mandatory and priority projects, how do you choose from the remainder – fairly and consistently? The answer is in numbers

You can compare benefit/cost by three types of contribution to corporate goals. For example:

- Strategic:
    - Directly contributes to corporate goals
    - Adds new revenue sources, products or services
    - Establishes new positioning
- Efficiency:
    - Increases production
    - Reduces costs
- Operational:
    - Equipment servicing to maintain output
    - System upgrades to match current technology

So, let's assume an arbitrary weighting scale of 100 points on the vertical scale. You have three major corporate concerns so you decide to assess the levels of these concerns as:

- Strategic projects: 65 to 100
- Efficiency projects: 30 to 70
- Operational projects: 1 to 35

You then assess each of your projects accordingly and plot these against a scale of relative cost, man-hours, or size. Use size if this implies high risk for a small organization or the swamping of resources to the detriment of other initiatives. Let's assume you select size. In this connection it is interesting to note that rather than a linear scale, a ratio scale is more useful simply because there are always more small projects than large. So, again with an arbitrary scale of 100, this time on the horizontal, you decide to assess your projects in the ranges:

- Very small project   1 - 5
- Small project   5 - 10
- Mid range project   10 - 25
- Large project   25 - 50
- An exceptionally large project   50 - 100

You then plot all your projects accordingly on a chart (Figure 13-2).

Plot all your results on a chart and use a secondary ranking if necessary

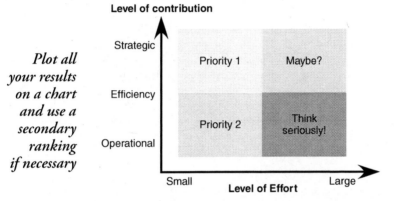

Figure 13-2: Chart showing format for ranking of projects

Secondary ranking

The process just described may not resolve all of the conflicts and priorities amongst your projects. Therefore, you may want to incorporate additional criteria to further reduce your selection. You can do this by drawing up a list of secondary criteria and allocating penalty or premium points to the projects in conflict. For example rank on the uncertainty spectrum of risk/opportunity.

Risks such as:

- Schedule risk
- Cost estimate accuracy risk
- Technological risk

Score these each, low to high: -1 to -10

Opportunities such as:

- Public relations
- Marketing

- Learning and competence

Score these each, low to high: +1 to +10

Another approach is on the basis of impacts and benefits, such as positive impact on organization:

In the last analysis, does the line up of projects "feel right"? If not, negotiate the last projects to be selected!

- Consequence of not doing
- Degree of urgency

Score these each, low to high: +1 to +10

Or benefits to the organization:

- Broadness of application
- Return on investment

Score these each, low to high: +1 to +10

Of course there are many other possibilities but you get the general idea. Finally, total up the points and discover which projects are the winners and losers. In all likelihood the result will not satisfy all concerned and the only thing left is to negotiate between the various stakeholders to arrive at what feels the most "comfortable". However, the process does serve to bring all the issues out into the open.

13.8   Next steps

The next steps in processing newly selected projects depend on their size, but in general:

In other words, move these projects into the first phase of the organization's standard project life span sequence

- Allocate "investigative" funding to fully develop the business case, or
- Fund a feasibility study, or
- Authorize the conceptual phase of the project to research the technology and its practicality

At the same time:

- Confirm the economics
- Estimate budget and resources required
- Identify risks and alternatives
- Sell concept and obtain approvals for each project to proceed.

You can learn more advanced selection approaches in the next chapter.

CHAPTER 14

Optimizing portfolio management

14.1 The need to better understanding suboptimal selection

Whenever resources are diverted from one project to another there is an inevitable reduction in efficiency

In Chapter 13 we discussed portfolio management in very simplistic terms. We looked at what portfolio management is, why it is needed, and some of the things that management needs to consider to make it work. In particular, we suggested a simple approach to project selection. However, for organizations with more than a few projects, the question of optimizing project selection requires a much more sophisticated view.

In the first place, it means moving beyond project management, or even program management, to the issue of optimizing alignment and value to the organization. In the second place, it means managing resources across a diverse and often disparate set of projects rather than have them compete on the basis of the "squeaky wheel". And yet, whenever resources are diverted from one project to another, there is the inevitable reduction in efficiency for the project that then ends up lower on the priority list.

Optimizing a fair number of projects in a portfolio is a significant mathematical challenge

Project effectiveness is still essential, but the issue of individual project efficiency now becomes one of impact of the realization of the collective benefits of the whole portfolio. Even assuming that we had all the data, the result is a complex mathematical challenge. Of course, we know that we can never have all the data because the required project data evolves through each project life span and is subject to change due to project risk and opportunity.

In a masterful series of papers, Lee Merkhofer, tackles the subject of project portfolio selection as a subject of vital interest to senior executives.[1] Lee approaches his topic from the perspective of why so many corporations fail to optimize their project portfolios and instead settle for an unacceptable "60% solution". Lee identifies five main reasons for this failure and provides recommendations for remedying each.

We are indebted to Lee for permission to include here this brief synopsis of the concepts taken from his series of papers. Make sure you read his full set of papers that can be found in the reference provided.

Introduction to the Lee Merkhofer approach

The "60% solution" can be improved by increasing value without increasing costs, or reducing costs without reducing value

At business conferences recently, business leaders and consultants have been talking about the "60% solution". Reportedly, 40% of the available value from business is lost due to errors in decision-making and weaknesses in business systems. Applying the concept to portfolio management, the challenge is to increase value by 20-40% without increasing costs, or decrease costs by 20-40% without decreasing value, by making better choices in each budget cycle.

The first step is to understand the reasons for suboptimal project selection.

14.2   Reason #1: Errors and bias in judgment

The fact that people's intuitive decisions are often strongly and systematically biased has been firmly established over the past 30 years by literally hundreds of empirical studies. Some of the principle biases and ways to counter them are described below.

Status quo bias

- Consider carefully whether this is the best choice or only the one most comfortable because it requires the least change

- Think about what your objectives are and whether they are best served by the status quo or a change

Sunk cost bias

- Seek the views of those not involved in the original choice

- How influenced are you by past investment?

- How much does sunk cost bias the decisions and recommendations of others?

- How willing are you to "cut your losses"? Even smart choices at the time can have bad outcomes.

Supporting evidence bias

- Are you examining all the evidence? Don't accept confirming evidence without question.

- Look for counter arguments, encourage people to take a "devil's advocate" view

- Are you being honest with yourself and your motives or just gathering information to help make a smart choice, or just seeking confirmation?

- Don't surround yourself with "yes men"

Framing Bias

- Are you working on the real problem?

- Try re-framing the problem in a neutral way or one that embraces different reference points

- Look at the problem from other perspectives, i.e., reverse the context. If seller, then as buyer, or vice versa.

- Look at the big picture, e.g., "What's the total cost of ownership?" not just "What's the price?"

- Similarly, look at collective portfolio risk, not just project-by-project

Estimating and Forecasting Biases

- Take a stab on your own before consulting others

- Seek opinions from multiple and diverse sources before exposing your own

- Ask for "realistic" estimates and ask for the underlying assumptions

- Ask for range estimates rather than single value best guesses

- In invited project proposals include a heading that calls for ways in which the product might fail

- Give people feedback on the outcomes of their estimates so they can improve their repository of knowledge

- Make sure that project proposals, or significant changes, are supported by network timeline logic and check lists to make sure that all activities are covered

- Use high-level quick-estimate logic to verify that "decimal points have not been misplaced"

14.3   Reason #2: Failure to see the forest for the trees

Most organizations put considerable effort into making individual projects successful. However, it should be obvious that it is the performance of the project portfolio as a whole that really matters. Many organizations simply do not manage the aggregate cost, value and risk of their whole project portfolio. Project managers tend to the individual "trees", but no one is caring for the "forest"!

Problems of project-by-project decision making

If project selection decisions are not made at the portfolio level, by default the project portfolio is the end result of individual project choices made one at a time with little regard for the impact that one project has on the next. Project-by-project decision-making leads to a bias toward short-duration, relatively low-value and low-risk efforts – and too many of them. The result is that resources are spread too thinly and further; multi-tasking reduces people's efficiency. Alternatively, when a large project does get started, available resources get sucked into the big one leaving the remainder high and dry.

Problems of lack of clear priorities

A related problem is the failure to establish organizational project priorities causing inefficiencies in the day-to-day allocation of project resources. Suppose you are a member of a project team in a typical organization working on several projects concurrently. Now, suppose you finish a milestone on an important project ahead of schedule. Do you use the opportunity to get an early start on your next task on this project? More likely, you turn your attention to one of your other projects, one belonging to the manager that you like best, has the most interesting projects, or writes your performance reviews.

Your day-to-day priorities are based on your desire to minimize the pressures you feel from the various project managers you serve. Although the organization may gain more from your taking the opportunity to put your important project ahead of schedule, that project is unlikely to benefit from your early finish because your organization has not established clear project priorities.

Enter the project portfolio database

Solving the problems created by project-by-project decision-making requires shifting the focus to the project portfolio. The first step is to collect information about individual projects into a common database. Here, all on-going and proposed projects of the organization are contained in a single project inventory.

The antidote to the "60% solution" is a database inventory of key data on all projects in the portfolio

Alternatively, multiple project inventories can be created representing project portfolios for different departments, programs, or businesses. Since project portfolio management can be conducted at any level, the choice of one portfolio versus many depends on the size of the organization and its structure. The key is to group projects using common resources so as to leverage knowledge and expertise needed for execution. If multiple project portfolios are defined, the groupings should be organized so as to be as independent of one another as possible.

Standard project reference information is obviously required in the database. More importantly, the data must include some level of business justification, risk assessment, and value and urgency calculation. A standard template should be devised to ensure the collection of requisite information in a common format.

Establish a portfolio management office

If the number of projects in the portfolio is significant, establish a *portfolio* management office (PMO) with responsibilities similar to those of the program management office we described in Chapter 12. Responsibility for the PMO must be in the hands of a project portfolio manager with considerable experience in managing projects. This person must also have the authority and stature to work with a steering committee of senior corporate executives.

A portfolio management office is necessary to manage the project assets

At the same time, this PMO manager must be provided with full control over the available resources, and authority to suspend commitment of investment dollars to any project at any time due to failure to make anticipated progress, changing economic climate, or shifts in business objectives.

There is a key difference between a program or project management office and a portfolio management office. The former are typically concerned with tracking progress, and time and costs to individual project completions. While this may also be true of a portfolio management office, this office must also estimate and track the value of the ensuing products. The collection of this data means holding a mandate well beyond the project life span and into the product life span.

14.4   Reason #3: Lack of the right metrics

The metrics that an organization uses have a big impact on the projects that get chosen. They also have an impact on what projects get proposed because managers interpret them as indicators of what the organization considers important. Therefore, lack of the right metrics can lead to choosing from the wrong projects

Inadequacy of financial metrics

The PMO must use the right metrics

Most organizations use financial metrics such as return on investment (ROI), return on assets (ROA), internal rate of return (IRR), net present value (NPV), payback period, and so on. The biggest limitation of such metrics for project prioritization is that they may not capture all of the organization's true objectives. As an obvious example, public-sector organizations have non-financial objectives such as protecting public health and the environment. These are beyond the reach of financial metrics. In the private sector the issue is shareholder value versus stakeholder value. Companies that evaluate projects by estimating impacts on profits alone ignore a significant component of market value.

Finding the right metrics by creating a value model

Organizations tend to measure what is easy to measure, not necessarily what is important, and most organizations use a bottom-up approach. Unless there is a way to combine metrics to determine the value added by projects, the metrics will not be of much help in identifying value-maximizing project portfolios. The answer is to create a value model using a top-down approach. The desired metrics are the inputs to the value model.

Building a value model is not as difficult as it may sound. Even a fairly sophisticated value model can be constructed in a 2-3 day framing workshop (using techniques based on multi-attribute utility analysis, influence diagramming, and causal modeling). The model captures the understanding of the organization's experts in relevant areas such as R&D, engineering, manufacturing, marketing, sales, customer relations, legal counsel, regulatory affairs, and so on. The value model establishes an explicit connection between the characteristics of the business that may be impacted by proposed projects and the value ultimately derived from them.

An organization-specific value model using the right metrics is necessary for intelligent decision making

Having a value model is critical to making intelligent project decisions. Project value determines whether the project should be done at all and, after it has been started, whether it should be continued. A good value model has other uses as well. It provides a way to estimate the value of a day of schedule, the value of a project feature, or the value of a dollar of project cost. The project team or portfolio manager can use the value model to illustrate how a marginal change in resources, say plus or minus 10%, might affect the overall value to be generated. A value model is a means for explaining and justifying the resources required for doing projects.

In the last analysis, every organization needs its own set of metrics and value model to be applied to all portfolios if multiple portfolios exist.

14.5 Reason #4: Inadequate attention to risk

Early attention to project risk is also an essential ingredient

When it comes to selecting projects many organizations still don't adequately address risk. More attention to project risk is needed because the increasingly competitive economic environment is putting tremendous pressure on managers to produce results faster. At the same time, projects are becoming more complex due to new technologies, more regulatory requirements, increased product liability, and the greater interdependency organizations have with multiple business partners and hence the number of stakeholders.

The level of risk management required obviously depends on the level of risk in each case. Riskier projects, such as new product launches, global initiatives, projects involving new technology, major regulatory-driven projects, and so forth, tend to have complex interacting elements and involve high stakes. A poor track record on similar projects is an indicator or risk. While risk management is most needed for the most risky projects, some level of project risk management must be provided in all cases. Project risk management is a well-trodden path for competent project managers.

However, certain types of risk need to be managed at the project selection level. War stories abound of projects successfully on-time and on-budget but the product was a disaster. Project portfolio management provides an opportunity to account for external risks and to get senior executives to take some ownership of project risks before the project commences.

Risky projects may be good projects

The organization must establish its level of risk tolerance

Alan Greenspan of the US Federal Reserve Board has observed: "Risk-taking is indeed a necessary condition for the creation of wealth".[2] So, a clear policy on corporate risk taking is essential. And, unless risk is measured, it is difficult to use it as a consideration for project selection. Hence, major risks including those relating to the product-in-use must be identified, their potential impacts estimated and assigned a probability. With the major risks thus quantified, the overall risk of the project portfolio can be determined.

Organizational risk tolerance

The degree of aversion to taking a major risk can be measured and expressed as a number called the risk tolerance. Risk tolerance is not the maximum amount that the decision maker can afford to lose on a project but rather; risk tolerance involves applying an adjustment that penalizes the value of a risky project.

Once risk tolerance has been established, the certain equivalent for any project can be obtained by subtracting a risk adjustment factor from the expected value of the uncertain future value to be derived from the project. The risk adjustment factor depends on the risk tolerance and the amount of project risk. An important advantage of this approach is that a single risk tolerance can be established for the organization. Use of the common risk tolerance ensures that risks are treated consistently, thus avoiding the common bias in which greater levels of risk aversion tend to be applied by lower-level managers.

14.6   Reason #5: Inability to find the "efficient frontier"

The goal for selecting projects is to pick project portfolios that create the greatest possible risk-adjusted value without exceeding the applicable constraint on available resources. Economists call the set of investments that create the greatest possible value at the least possible cost the "efficient frontier." Most organizations fail to find the best project portfolios and, therefore, do not create all of the value available.

Definition of the efficient frontier

Suppose that an organization is currently conducting a set of projects represented by portfolio A as shown in Figure 14-1. Portfolio A is inefficient because there is another project portfolio B that produces more value for the same cost. Similarly, there is also a portfolio C that produces the same value for less cost. Furthermore, there is a portfolio D with a combination of both characteristics.

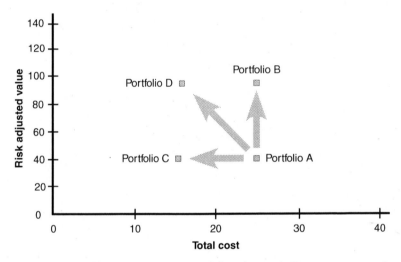

Figure 14-1: Different project portfolios have different costs and values

Now suppose we consider all possible portfolios that can be constructed from a set of project proposals. Typically there are many and Figure 14-2 shows a case where the organization had 30 project proposals under consideration in one budget cycle.

In practice, four of the thirty projects were considered mandatory (3 process fixes and a new initiative required by regulators) leaving 26 discretionary projects. In general, if there are N potential projects, there are 2^N possible project portfolios because there are a total of 2^N subsets within a set of N items.[3] Thus, this application required evaluating 2^{26} or approximately 67 million portfolios, far more than shown in Figure 14-2. The best portfolios define the efficient frontier.

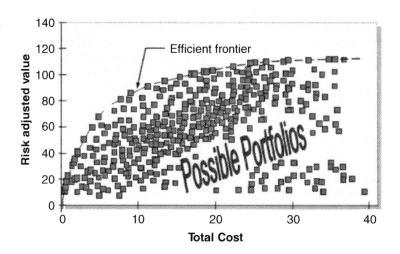

Figure 14-2: The best project portfolios define the efficient frontier

Create the "best bang for the buck" – but you'll need a computer program

Notice how the efficient frontier is curved, not straight. This is because the efficient frontier is made up of the best possible projects in the least-cost portfolios, i.e., those portfolios that are closest to the frontier boundary. These portfolios create the greatest "bang-for-the-buck". As the cost constraint is relaxed and more projects can be added, the new projects are not quite as good as those included earlier. The slope of the curve encompassing these projects is flatter because their bang-for-the-buck is not quite as high. Thus, there is a declining return in the value obtained with each additional increment of cost, hence the shape.

With a computer running an efficient optimization engine, it is relatively easy to locate the efficient frontier using the right algorithms. However, these algorithms must be set to determine how the costs and benefits of individual projects combine to determine the costs and benefits of the project portfolio as a whole. In simple situations where projects are independent and risks are either independent or do not matter, the costs and value of the project portfolio are basically just sums of the costs and values of the individual projects. However, if there are interdependencies or a need to adjust for risks, more sophisticated models are required.

14.7   Finding the efficient frontier adds value

If we locate the efficient frontier then, for any specified total port-folio cost, we can pick the specific project portfolio that produces the greatest possible value. Figure 14-3, derived from an actual ap-plication, shows that an alternative portfolio was found that in-creased value by over 30% without increasing costs. Similarly, an alternative portfolio was found that reduced costs by 40% without decreasing value. This result is typical. Application of the efficient frontier approach shows that current project portfolios are often well below their potential.

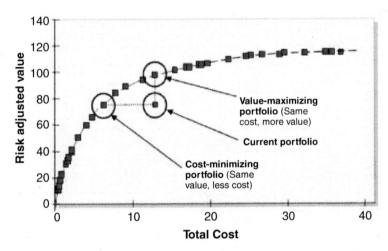

Figure 14-3: Project portfolio enhanced by applying the efficient frontier

The efficient frontier moves over time

The efficient frontier is not static. Better project options shift the balance

Note that the efficient frontier is not static. Organizations face the challenge of finding project alternatives that advance the frontier. As project managers better understand the link between their proj-ect designs and the value derived by the organization they create better project proposals. Moreover, better technology creates new opportunities that create more value for less cost. Hence the ef-ficient frontier moves up over time, but the goal remains the same – create as much value as possible using as little capital as possible using the efficient frontier.

14.8   Five levels of project portfolio management maturity

Figure 14-4 summarizes five levels of portfolio management maturity. Each level represents the adoption of one of the major solutions for addressing the reasons that organizations choose the wrong projects, as discussed in this chapter.

Level 1:

- Organizes the work into discrete projects and tracks costs and other resource usage at the project level.

Level 2:

- Replaces project-by-project decision making with identification of the best collection of projects to be conducted within the resources available. At a minimum, this requires aggregating project data into a central database, assigning responsibilities for project portfolio management, and forced ranking projects.

Level 3:

- Requires developing metrics, models, and tools for estimating the value to be derived from projects. Although interdependencies are still ignored, this allows projects to be accurately ranked by "bang-for-the-buck" and provides a good approximation of the value-maximizing project portfolio.

Level 4:

- Improves the tools to correctly account for project risks and interdependencies enabling the project portfolio to be optimized

Level 5:

- Puts processes in place for continuous learning and improvement with project portfolio management as a core competency

14.9   Summary of what organizations need to do

✓ *Address the errors and biases that affect human judgment*

- Increase awareness of prevalent errors and biases, including comfort zone, perception, and motivation biases, as well as errors in reasoning, and "group think"
- Consider incentives and the effects of framing when evaluat-

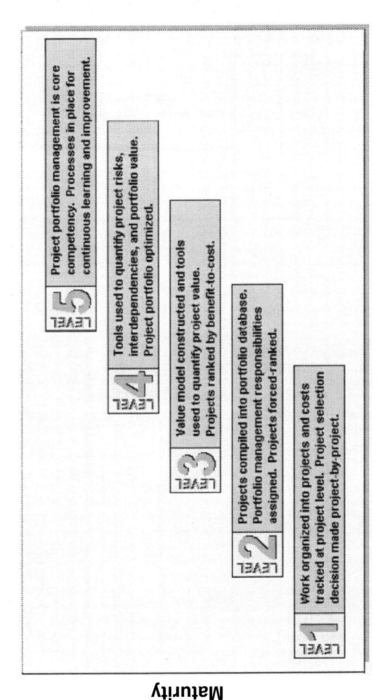

Figure 14-4: Five levels of project portfolio management
(Reprodced with permission)

ing your own and other people's judgments. Remember that an estimate from a disinterested but knowledgeable party may be more reliable than that of a better-informed but involved expert.

- Provide feedback to people on the accuracy of their forecasts. Collect data from funded projects to help calibrate people's estimates and keep them honest.

✓ *Get control of the project selection process*

- See the forest as well as the trees. Collect projects and project proposals into a common database. Look for duplications and interdependencies. Establish a common proposal format and content.

- Move from project-by-project decision-making to decision-making aimed at producing optimal project portfolios. Create a project portfolio management office with responsibility for managing the organization's portfolio of projects.

- Understand the options that are created and destroyed by project choices. When choosing projects consider project urgency as well as project value.

✓ *Develop an enterprise view of project value*

- Create a value model for your business, one that documents best-organizational understanding about how projects create value

- Use the value model to develop metrics and to estimate the impacts of doing projects

- Engage senior executives in the process of establishing objectives, defining how value tradeoffs should be made, sharing ownership of project decisions, and co-developing project expectations

✓ *Be proactive in addressing risk*

- Establish processes for identifying internal and external project risks, communicating those risks, and implementing risk-mitigation action plans

- Avoid the bias toward doing too many, mostly low-risk, low-return projects. Remember that risky projects often create learning and increased capability, values that aren't readily captured in financial metrics.

- For "big bet" investments quantify risks and consider establishing an organizational risk tolerance to guide decision-making

✓ *Get to the efficient frontier by institutionalizing decision making competencies*

- Promote and attend training workshops on the logical principles of decision analysis, project prioritization, and capital budgeting

- Learn the best techniques for articulating objectives, expressing value tradeoffs, assessing probabilities, and establishing risk tolerance

- Recognize and reward people based on the quality of their decisions, not just based on the quality of their outcomes

- Identify and use the best-available tools

The 60% solution can be beaten! It may not be easy, but it can be done. The fact that optimizing project decisions is hard to do, but doable, is how organizations gain significant competitive business advantage and become more successful.

References

[1] Merkhofer, Dr. M.W. (Lee), *Choosing the Wrong Portfolio of Projects: And what your organization can do about it*, a series of six papers published in the guest papers section at http://www.maxwideman.com, 2003

[2] Kahaner, L., and A. Greenspan, *The Quotations of Chairman Greenspan*, Adams Media Corporation, 2000

[3] See the paper: *Mathematics: Methods for Solving the Capital Allocation Problem* at http://www.prioritysystem.com (Accessed 8/7/04)

Part V Final Thoughts

CHAPTER 15

Focus on success

15.1 What is project success?

"On time, on budget" is no longer a sufficient measure of project success

Do we mean project success, or do we really mean project management success; do we just mean "on time and under budget" or "customer satisfaction"? Is this something we can measure or is it a matter of perception? We might observe here that in the real world perception is reality, and this measure of success depends largely on the quality of the product, something that will be remembered long after "on time and under budget" are buried in last year's financial statements!

So, there are lots of ways at looking at success as we shall see in the next section. Of course the project team wants to be seen as having made a successful effort, it is a part of their sense of satisfaction. However, the blunt truth is that how we got there is of little concern to the customer. The customer's success measure is the timely product value to them minus the cost to produce.

But in the bigger picture of today's world we suggest that:

Project success is the extent to which its product creates new benefits at least cost to the environment

Our "environment" is our "collective commons"

However, what do we mean by "environment" in this case? We mean our collective commons consisting of the global space we live in, the land, oceans, air, and so on, as well as the cultural environment that reflects our quality of life.

That's a tall order, but it should be a part of our professional ethic.

15.2 A little bit of history

The 1987 definition of project management that we quoted in

Chapter 2 identified five objectives. These consisted of the four basic functional objectives of scope, quality, time and cost, and a fifth objective of a different dimension that we identified as customer satisfaction. What is the basis?

Interest in project management stems from a desire to manage projects better and to end up with a project that is more successful. But how do we determine when a project is successful? Well, some things can be measured but for the most part it becomes a matter of opinion.

Presumably, for a favorable opinion to be formed by those associated with a project, they must first be reasonably satisfied with it. But then it is a question of whose opinion, or whose opinion should take precedence? Here again we have a dilemma because success can be measured on at least two levels – the opinion of those who are satisfied with the project management *process*, and those who are satisfied with its *product.*

The trouble with measuring the level of satisfaction with the project management **process** is that there are usually many participants involved and each of them views it from their personal perspective. So, perhaps a successful project is one in which all the participants are about equally satisfied (proportional to their involvement). But the project team's perception of success is always going to be subject to a certain amount of bias. After all, their jobs may be on the line![1] Of course, the cynic might say that the really successful project is one in which all the participants are about equally **dis**satisfied!

Then there is the question of measuring the success of the **product**. When do you measure that? It is obviously not measurable until the project's product has had some exposure in the marketplace and that may be long after the project itself is completed. But at least at some time we should be able to measure market reaction or, if the product is targeted to a particular group of customers, we should be able to measure **customer** satisfaction.

If you look at these two closely, success of the process and success of the product, you will notice that the former really reflects the internal performance of the project, i.e., the **internal** environment, while the latter reflects the **external** environment. We discussed the internal and external environments in Chapters 9 and 11. These concepts are shown diagrammatically in Figure 15-1.

Project success can be measured by metrics, but often it is a matter of opinion

Project success can be measured on two levels: the process and the product

There is also the question of when you measure success

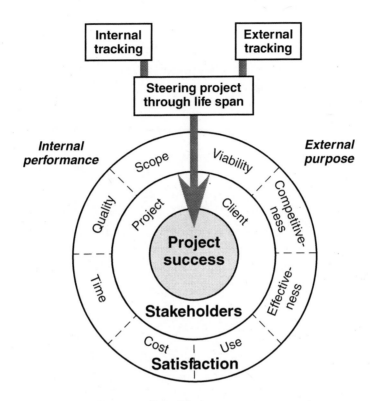

Figure 15-1: The success target

As we mentioned in Chapter 3, in the project management literature there is the idea of the "triple constraint", sometimes known
as the "iron triangle". This usually comprises the three elements:
budget, schedule, and performance. But authors differ and the
three sides of the triangle might be labeled any of scope, quality,
time (schedule), cost (budget), or resources – pick any three, you
choose! Unfortunately, there are still many authors who cling to
this limited construct.

*The so-called
"triple
constraint" or
"iron triangle"
is a limited
and obsolete
construct*

Whichever triangle you choose, it is clearly not an accurate ba-
rometer of ultimate project success. If nothing else, the quality of
the product, which is also a reflection of the quality of the work
that went into the project and its product, transcends all the others. Still, a big problem remains. It is a common observation that
perceived success varies depending upon who does the perceiving,
and at what point in time success is being evaluated.

Projects can overrun time and budget and still be great commercial successes. But you must know whether you have that luxury!

In the literature there are many examples of projects that heavily overran budget and schedule yet were subsequently considered great commercial successes. While others meeting the "triple constraint" proved to be downright failures. Perhaps the differences can be found in changes in the external environmental conditions, such as changes in the market or in customer attitudes. In other words, the products of a project may provide only partial satisfaction in response to the sponsor's originally stated project needs.

This may well be because every project is a part of a larger picture as we discussed in Chapter 5. In many cases, this "larger picture" becomes clearer as the project proceeds, leading to better understood needs. This is especially true of the more technologically advanced projects such as software development or research and development. The answer in these cases seems to be "proceed by iteration" as we described in Chapter 5. The moral is:

> *Doing the wrong thing right is never a success, but doing the right thing even half right could still be a winner!*

15.3   Can project success be measured?

To believe that we can objectively measure the entire spectrum of success may be something of an illusion.

If the only objectives of the project are to get it completed within scope, cost and schedule, then certainly degrees of success can be measured against these parameters. But, as discussed above, if the real objective is to end up with a successful project then, important though these are, they are not the ultimate determinants of success. Heresy? Perhaps. But success, a difficult notion at best, depends on realizing satisfied customers!

In fact, when measuring project success, perhaps we should consider the objectives of all stakeholders throughout the project life span and at all levels in the management hierarchy. Therefore, with such a multitude of objectives, to believe that we can objectively measure the entire spectrum of success of a project may be somewhat of an illusion.[2]

Too often in the past, project managers have assumed that by concentrating on the internal efficiency issues they get the project out of the door on time and under budget and so have achieved success. This attitude is actually dangerous for project organizations that live or die by their ability to satisfy their customers.[3] At the very least, the importance of developing and updating the client's

In the end, success may depend on whether what the client asks for is what they really need

views in planning and assessing project success should not be overlooked. Perhaps equally important is the development of the client's requirements in a way that ensures that what the client asks for is what they really need.

In the long run, what really matters is whether the parties associated with and affected by a project are satisfied. Good schedule and cost performance alone means very little in the face of a poorly performing and poorly received end product.[4]

15.4   Four dimensions of project success

In 1995, Shenhar, Dvir and Levy published the results of extensive research into the subject of project success,[5] updating earlier work by Pinto.[6] For their purposes, Shenhar et al defined project success as:[7]

> "A strategic management concept where project efforts must be aligned with the strategic long-term goals of the organization."

As they observe:

Surprisingly, a documented baseline is frequently missing from most projects

> "The intent is to establish appropriate expectations of both top management and the project team prior to project initiation. These expectations then provide a baseline for both the project launch decision and the inevitable trade-off decisions required of project management during the project. Surprisingly, a documented baseline such as this is frequently missing from most projects."

The research revealed four distinct primary categories (principal success criteria) as seen at project completion. The authors describe these as follows.[8]

1. Internal project objectives (efficiency during the project)

- How successful was the project team in meeting its schedule objectives?

- How successful was the project team in meeting its budget objectives?

- How successful was the project team in managing any other resource constraints?

2. Benefit or value to customer (effectiveness in the short term)

- Did the product meet its specified requirements of functional performance and technical standards?
- What was the project's impact on the customer, and what did the customer gain?
- Does the customer actually use the product, and are they satisfied with it?
- Does the project's product fulfill the customer's needs, and/or solve the problem?
- Note that the value to the customer may be real or perceived and a physical asset or an intellectual asset.

3. Direct contribution (in the medium term)

- Has the new or modified product become an immediate business and/or commercial success, has it enhanced immediate revenue and profits?
- Has it created a larger market share?

4. Future opportunity (in the long term)

- Has the project created new opportunities for the future, has it contributed to positioning the organization consistent with its vision, goals?
- Has it created a new market or new product potential, or assisted in developing a new technology?
- Has it contributed additional capabilities or competencies to the receiving organization?

Most measurable project success criteria are time dependent

These principal success criteria are summarized in Figure 15-2.

An examination of the measurable success criteria reveals that they are clearly time-dependent as shown in Figure 15-3.

Anecdotal evidence also indicates that the perception of success changes with time depending on the elapsed time from completion. For example, a project could have its principal focus on creating future opportunity (Category 4). Such a project is unlikely to be viewed as successful until such time as those opportunities have actually materialized. Similarly, users may be resistant to a new system or software until they become familiar and comfortable with it and appreciate its advantages.

Success Category	Measurable Success Criteria
1. Internal Project Objectives (Pre-completion)	- Meeting schedule - Within budget - Other resource constraints met - The project team is satisfied with their efforts
2. Benefit to Customer (Short term)	- Meeting functional performance - Meeting technical specifications & standards - Favorable impact on customer, customer's gain - Fulfilling customer's needs - Solving a customer's problem - Customer is using product - Customer expresses satisfaction
3. Direct Contribution (Medium term)	- Immediate business and/or commercial success - Immediate revenue and profits enhanced - Larger market share generated
4. Future Opportunity (Long term)	- Will create new opportunities for future - Will position customer competitively - Will create new market - Will assist in developing new technology - Has, or will, add capabilities and competencies

Figure 15-2: Summary of principle success criteria

The timing of success measurement should bet set in the project's business case

How much time you should allow depends on the project and the situation. While the time interval probably varies widely from industry to industry and project to project, it may not be too difficult to set the time for a given project. Ideally, this should be stated in the business case for the project and under the heading of key success indicators.

15.5 Project success criteria

Critical Success Factors and Key Success Indicators are not the same thing

Although by no means universal practice, it really is essential that the project's success criteria be clearly defined and agreed before significant development is initiated. These success criteria may be defined in a number of different ways, for example: "business objectives or goals", "technical requirements" or other labels including the word "success".[9] In our view, it is useful to identify *critical success factors* (CSFs) and *key success indicators* (KSIs) and distinguish between them so that they are not the same thing. These two terms are described below.

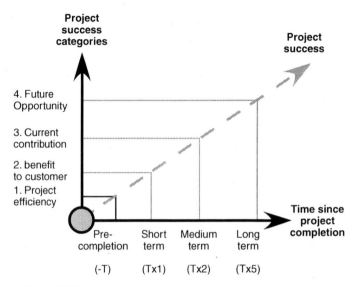

Note: Time "T" is a suggested yardstick based on the time taken in the execution phase of the project. Actual intervals will depend on the industry involved.

RMW © 11/10/01

Figure 15-3: Project success varies with time

Critical success factors (CSF)

A *factor* is something that either exists or it doesn't, in our case in the project environment. So we define *critical success factors* as:

Those observable factors, listed in order of importance, that when present in the project's environment are most conducive to the achievement of a successful project

Examples of favorable factors include:

If the CSF's are not favorable, you may want to have nothing to do with the project

- Project objectives aligned with corporate mission
- Top management support
- A corporate culture of open communication
- The characteristics of the project manager or team leader
- Absence of destructive power and politics
- Favorable environment, especially towards reception of the project and its product
- The perception of urgency and importance of satisfactory project completion

These CSFs are generally factors beyond the control of the project team, are difficult to quantify and don't change much. Nevertheless, their presence improves the chances of project success while their absence militates against it.

Key success indicators (KSI)

Key success indicators may also be known as key performance indicators (KPI), key requirements areas (KRA) or just success criteria as we saw in the previous section. These may refer to the internal performance of the project's management. Or they may refer to the things that reflect the corporate decision for selecting the project in the first place, based on the ultimate benefits to be derived from the product of the project. For purposes of clearly distinguishing between CSFs and KPIs, we take the latter view.

Hence, we define *key success indicators* as:

Those project management indicators that:

- *Are determined at the beginning of the project and listed in order of priority*

- *Reflect directly on the key objectives of the project, i.e., the expected benefits of the product, and*

- *Provide the basis for project management trade off decisions during the course of the project*

And, after completion of the project:

- *Are most likely to result in acceptance of the project and its product by the project's stakeholders as being successful in terms of customer satisfaction, and*

- *Can be measured in some way, at some time, on some scale*

Key success indicators can and should be quantified and measured after project completion

Unlike CSFs, KSIs can and should be quantified, i.e., measured, because the impacts of KSIs are things that the project team can influence. The project team should set their sights on KSIs, especially when making trade off decisions during the course of the project life span. However, you must also recognize that KSIs can and do change as the project progresses, which is why it is so important to keep an eye on the project environment as we discussed in Chapters 9 and 11.

15.6   A self-test for project success

The following questions suggest a useful self-test for the project manager who takes pride in a successful project.[10] Each question may be rated on a scale of, say, 1 to 7, with the best projects taking the highest total marks! The overall intent is to determine the extent to which the project objectives are identified, reviewed and met.

Internal issues

This project:

1. Will meet/has met its defined scope

2. Will conform/has conformed to its quality requirements

3. Will/has come in on schedule

4. Will/has come in on budget

5. As being developed, this project looks as if it will work (or did work as developed)

6. Given the problem for which it is intended, it appears to be the best choice amongst the alternatives available

7. Will provide/has provided results representing definite improvement over clients' previous conditions

External issues

1. The intended clients will/do make use of this project's product

2. Other important clients, i.e., those directly affected by the project, will/do make use of it

3. We are confident that non-technical start-up problems will be/were minimal because the project will be/was accepted by its intended clients

4. We are/were satisfied with the process by which the product/facility is/was being brought into existence

5. This project benefited/will benefit the intended clients directly through increased user efficiency or effectiveness

6. Use of this project will lead/has led to improved, or more effective, decision-making or performance by its intended clients

7. This project will/did have a positive impact on all of its stakeholders

15.7   Vision, creativity, discovery and judgment[11]

Good advice for project managers and their teams:

Vision:

The project manager and his or her team must have a clear mental picture of the outcome of their project at all times. They must develop an understanding of all the steps involved in getting there, and their logical sequence. It is just as well to have a good picture of the characteristics of the environment in which the project is being launched and the impact that the project will have on that environment.

Creativity:

During the life of a project the project team will face many ideas, suggestions and hurdles. Even more solutions will appear and disappear in chaotic piles of data and a jumble of contradictory statistics and reports of expert opinions. Each offers its own merits, assumptions, limitations and risks. Managers need to cut through the chaos to reach a solution appropriate to the project, often with insufficient or incomplete information. The key rests in his/or her ability to think creatively in each situation and to act boldly.

Discovery:

In the course of a project, but especially in the planning phases, there is often a real need to explore new ideas relevant to the project. In these phases, ideas should be openly suggested, tested and improved with little risk. The resulting discovery should be assessed against what is important in terms of project success.

Judgment:

Appraisal and deduction are intrinsic elements of an individual's decision-making process that is inevitably influenced by circumstantial factors such as:

- Self-image, including irrelevant emotions and sometimes distorted impressions of one's own capabilities

- Judgment by others taken for granted, but which itself requires distinction between emotional blame or criticism and clear, rational assessment; and

- Collective judgments that act to restrict the leader's freedom of action.

Together, these attributes can act to focus constructive energies towards real project needs. They can also act to generate curiosity and the courage to try new ideas or take calculated risks in the project environment.

Conversely, an absence of these things can inhibit the project team from achieving the highest levels of project success.

In the end, project success probably depends most on taking the broadest possible view of project management

For the project manager and his or her team, project success depends to a considerable degree on a keen awareness, a rational analysis of current organizational circumstances, designing and taking the necessary steps to create and maintain a viable all-encompassing project plan, and faithfully executing its content.

References

[1] Pinto, J., summary provided by letter 6/5/89

[2] de Wit, A., *Measurement of Project Success*, International Journal of Project Management, Vol 6 No 3, August 1988, p164

[3] Pinto, J., summary provided in letter 6/5/89

[4] Baker, B.N., D. C. Murphy & D. Fisher, *Factors Affecting Project Success*, in *Project Management Handbook*, NY: Van Nostrand Reinhold, 1983, p669-685

[5] Shenhar, A.J., D. Dvir, & O. Levy, *Project Success: A Multidimensional Strategic Concept*, Research paper, MN: University of Minnesota, June 1995

[6] Pinto, J.K., & J. E. Prescott, *Planning and Tactical Factors in the Project Implementation Process*, Working Paper 89-07, University of Maine, December 1988

[7] Shenhar, A.J., & R.M. Wideman, *Improving PM: Linking Success Criteria to Project Type*, Southern Alberta PMI Chapter Symposium, Calgary, Alberta, May 1996

[8] Ibid.

[9] Thiry, M., contributed by Email, 5/31/04

[10] Pinto, J.K., & D. P. Slevin, adapted from *Project Success: Definitions and Measurement Techniques*, Project Management Journal, Vol XIX, PA: Project Management Institute, February 1988, p72

[11] Zuberi, Z., thoughts contributed by letter 6/5/90

CHAPTER 16

The future of project management

16.1 Will project management survive?

Over a decade ago, when I wrote the original version of this book, there was some concern whether project management would survive. There was some thought that it might be some passing management fad that, like so many before it, would be supplanted by some new approach. Well, so far it has not happened nor, it seems, is it likely to happen.

Projects have been around even before the building of the Great Pyramids in Egypt and there will always be projects. Indeed, the number and rate of projects is increasing steadily. So, the issue is not whether the project management discipline will survive, but rather in what form.

16.2 Internal issues

A number of concerns were expressed about the project management body of knowledge at the beginning of the 1990s. Some of them have still not been satisfactorily resolved, and hence represent a fruitful area of project management research. They are presented in the following sections.

Project management model

Although we have presented a number of different models of project management in this book, no single one has gained broad acceptability across the project management practitioner community. This is because there is still considerable disagreement about what project management is, how it works and how much it encompasses – from the very narrow to the very broad.

Project life span

The project life span is the most fundamental element of project management

The most fundamental element of project management, the project life span, is still poorly understood, poorly applied and under-represented in the project management literature. Perhaps this is because there must necessarily be a diversity of project life spans to suit different areas of project management application – and indeed individual projects.

Still, we think that at some level it should be possible to gain general acceptance of a generic model such as the one we've proposed.

Project management terminology

Lack of a commonly understood terminology is a real problem

It would be nice to believe that we could eliminate misunderstandings in project management communications by agreeing on a common glossary of terms. However, while ever people have different perceptions of the contents and mechanics of project management, they are just as equally likely to have differences in their understanding of the corresponding terminology.

Just as there are many dialects of the English language, there will be many shades of meanings of identical terms, similar meanings for different terms, as well as terms used in different contexts. And that is not taking into account the matter of translation into different languages.

The application of project management sub-disciplines

A well-established generic methodology could be an advantage

The publication of the Project Management Institute's *A Guide to the Project Management Body of Knowledge* has achieved a considerable improvement in the consistency of content presentation. However, the Guide is a ***descriptive*** document, i.e., it explains ***what the content is*** of each of the functional areas, i.e., the sub-disciplines, of project management. However, it does not explain ***how to do*** project management, even though some people try very hard to make it into a prescriptive document.

There are some good methodologies out there, and some good books on methodology, mostly focused on specific areas of project management application. However, there is by no means any consensus on what a generic methodology would look like. Given the number and variety of projects, perhaps such an expectation is unreasonable.

Still, we might see an improvement in project performance if there was greater consistency of approach and, of course, the place to start would be with the project life span at the executive control level!

16.3   External issues

Environmental factors

For projects to be successful, customers and users must buy-in to the product

There is increasing recognition that projects do not take place in isolation, even though some large projects seem to be run that way. Increasingly, attention must be paid to the environment. Here we are speaking of the environment in which the project takes place and into which the product is launched. That includes both the physical and the political environments.

These days, project participants and the public are more politically aware and active. A project team that does not take this into consideration is likely to encounter considerable difficulty when it comes time to launch the product into the care, custody and control of the customers or users. Whether their objections are reasonable or not, they will simply not buy in to the consequent changes.

Project management knowledge and competency

Not everyone is suited to project work, let alone being in charge

Considerable effort has been expended in the last decade to establish more effective ways of testing knowledge and competency. Great strides have been made through the efforts of some academics, institutions and even regulatory bodies. Still, much more work needs to be done to reach any degree of consensus in these areas.

In our view, perhaps one missing dimension is that some people are simply not suited to working in a project environment, let alone leading a project as a project manager. Establishing criteria in that direction might be helpful. We suspect that the problem is that there are far more projects these days than there are people who have the most suitable disposition to run them.

Breadth of project management

Project management encompasses program and portfolio managements

Has the term "project management" become a popular catchall word designed to attract attention? Should it focus solely on what it seems to imply, the management of a project, or should it also encompass program management, the management of several related projects, and project portfolio management, the management of a disparate group of projects with some shared constraints such as resources or financing.

In our view, this is a legitimate extension because of the impact of the larger scheme of things on the workings of an individual project. In fact it is part of the project environment for many projects.

Fundamental principles of project management

Are there fundamental or first principles of project management? In our view, there are but they have not been clearly enunciated by those with some authority in these matters.

We believe that if some agreement could be reached on a set of principles of project management, such as those we've presented in this book, then some of the foregoing problems would rapidly disappear. Certainly it would greatly facilitate alignment among the various project management organizations and their respective materials.

Who should be the custodians of project management knowledge?

Just because everyone is doing it doesn't mean that it is the best thing to do

Traditionally, academia has been the custodian of the knowledge represented by a discipline. In science this is achieved by careful research, documentation, the presentation of papers, discussion and updating. However, as we noted in Chapter 2, project management is as much an art as it is a science and as such needs individual practitioner input of what works, what doesn't, when and why.

The collection of "best practices", while a current popular corporate and academic pastime, is not necessarily the answer. Just because everyone is doing it does not mean it is the best thing to do or even the right thing to do. This is where a robust model of project management would be helpful, to identify where there are gaps in both our knowledge and our practice.

16.4   Areas of project management application

At present, projects seem to be classified by industry and that leads to a very large number. But how many different areas of project management application are there really? Of course, the answer to the question depends on the criteria you use to differentiate. Let us suppose the criteria are set such that we are looking at differences in the most suitable **style of management**. That is to say, ones that share a common basis for education and training in terms of approach. Then, if the problem of differing terminology is overlooked, and perhaps even the problem of snobbery, the number of really different types of project is probably quite small.

Indeed, in a paper titled *Toward a Fundamental Differentiation between Project Types*[1] we suggested that there are really only four, based on the premise that:

Different types of project work need to be managed differently

For a project to be successful, different types of project work associated with different types of product need to be managed differently.

In production there are two types of work: brainwork or brawn work. There are also two types of product: tangible, as in a physical asset, or intangible, as in an intellectual product such as software. As shown in Figure 16-1, this leads to:

1. A *tangible-craft* project such as traditional construction

2. A *tangible-intellectual* project such as the development of an all-new environmentally benign automobile

3. An *intangible-craft* project such as the routine updating of a procedures manual, or

4. An *intangible-intellectual* project such as a new theory or all-

		Tangible	Intangible
Type of Work in the Project	**Intellect**	**Example:** Development of an all electric car	**Example:** Development of a new theory
	Craft	**Example:** Detailing and construction of a building	**Example:** Updating a procedures manual
		Tangible	**Intangible**

Type of Product from the Project

new software

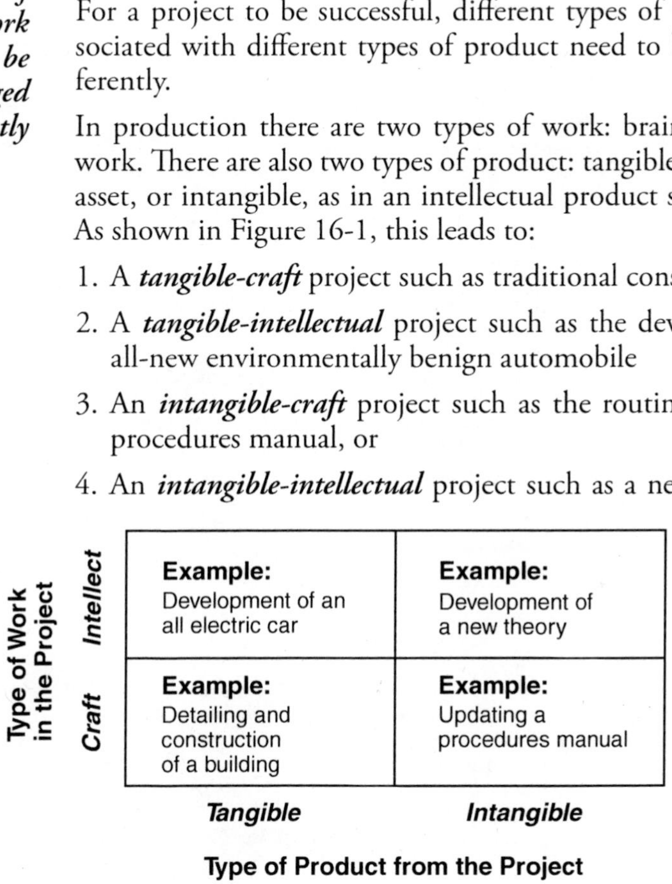

Figure 16-1: Basic 2x2 project classification

The characteristics of each of the four types are shown in Figure 16-2.

If we could narrow down the project management field like this, and focus on these four areas, then we might solve so many problems for so many industries!

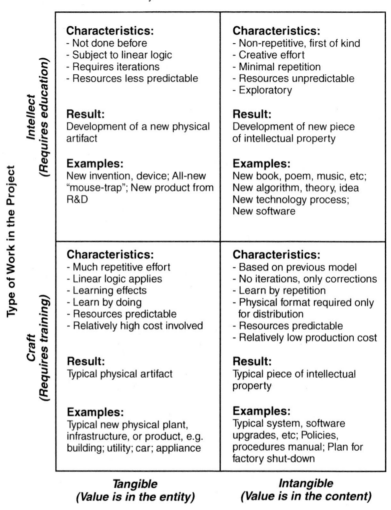

Figure 16-2: Basic project or major project component classification[2]

16.5 The future for the project manager

For the right kind of person, a project management career is a very attractive proposition because the future project manager will be a businessperson.

The future project manager-businessperson will be:

- One who will have the ability to appreciate and use technology advantageously

Projects will abound with plenty of opportunity for aspiring project managers

- One who will understand the needs of people in whatever social setting exists

Also:

- Worldwide projects will be directed towards new infrastructure, industrialization, consumer goods, and basic needs

- Domestic projects in the western world will stress infrastructure renovation and restoration, high-technology, environmental protection, defense, and space programs

- The project-driven organization will recognize the authority of the project manager, and from the ranks, select the executives of tomorrow.[3]

In short, if you fit the description, go for it!

References

[1] Shenhar, A.J. & R.M. Wideman: *Toward a Fundamental Differentiation between Project Types*, PICMET'97 at http://www.maxwideman.com/papers/differentiation/abstract.htm

[2] Ibid.

[3] Loweree, J.H., *Project Management: A Reference for Professionals*, Marcel Dekker, Inc., 1989, p1086

Appendices

Appendix A

Institutional goals and project management knowledge

A.1   Institutional goals

The Project Management Institute was the first organization assembled to concentrate on the subject of project management. It was launched in 1969 as a non-profit organization and its history tells us that the original focus was on scheduling project activities. In those days, personal computers had not been heard of and any computations had either to be done laboriously by hand, or almost as laboriously on massive and expensive mainframe computers.

Project management knowledge ranges from today's good practice to tomorrow's advanced concepts

Subsequently, the Institute's mandate was broadened to a dedication to advancing the state-of-the-art in the management of projects generally. Since then various other organizations have been established around the world with similar goals.

Such a mission involves the identification and articulation, development and sharing of relevant information amongst the membership. Since the "art and science" of project management is essentially the accumulated experience of its practitioners, it is important that open two-way communication is maintained if the field is to advance.

Figure A-1 displays diagrammatically the broad hierarchy of purpose of a typical project management institution.

In particular, the figure shows that project management knowledge may be represented by a spectrum ranging from current practice through to advanced research and development. However, the main focus is on an integrated body of knowledge that encompasses generally accepted good program and project management practice. Nevertheless, what may be considered good practice today may well be superseded in the future.

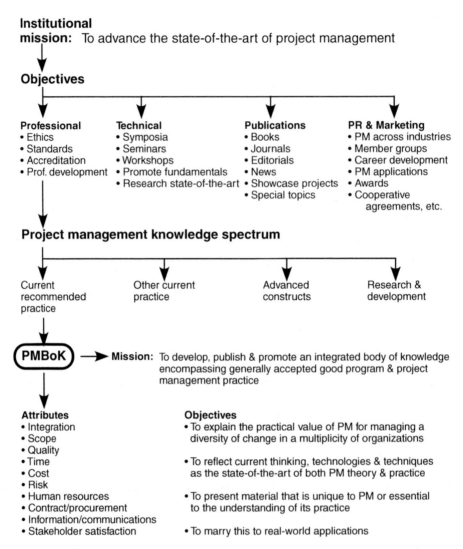

Institutional mission: To advance the state-of-the-art of project management

Objectives

Professional	**Technical**	**Publications**	**PR & Marketing**
• Ethics	• Symposia	• Books	• PM across industries
• Standards	• Seminars	• Journals	• Member groups
• Accreditation	• Workshops	• Editorials	• Career development
• Prof. development	• Promote fundamentals	• News	• PM applications
	• Research state-of-the-art	• Showcase projects	• Awards
		• Special topics	• Cooperative agreements, etc.

Project management knowledge spectrum

Current recommended practice	Other current practice	Advanced constructs	Research & development

PMBoK → **Mission:** To develop, publish & promote an integrated body of knowledge encompassing generally accepted good program & project management practice

Attributes
- Integration
- Scope
- Quality
- Time
- Cost
- Risk
- Human resources
- Contract/procurement
- Information/communications
- Stakeholder satisfaction

Objectives
- To explain the practical value of PM for managing a diversity of change in a multiplicity of organizations
- To reflect current thinking, technologies & techniques as the state-of-the-art of both PM theory & practice
- To present material that is unique to PM or essential to the understanding of its practice
- To marry this to real-world applications

Figure A-1: Conceptual institution project management mission

Still, if current practice is to advance, the remainder of the knowledge spectrum must receive attention and, over time, feed into the generally accepted body of project management knowledge. Moreover, there will be areas of project management application wherein other practices are appropriate, but which are not necessarily considered to be universally applicable.

A three-tier concept for the scope of project management knowledge consisting of "generally applicable", "industry-specific" and "the outputs from institutes of higher learning" is shown in Figure A-2.

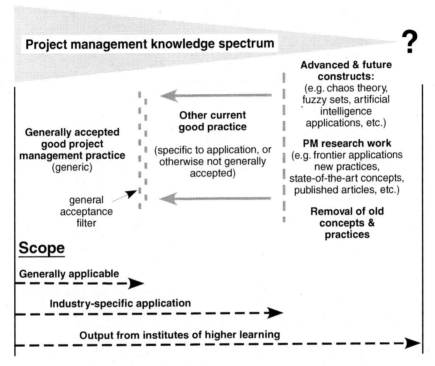

Figure A-2: Idealized progressive project management learning

A.2   Terms of reference for a body of knowledge

It is not easy to reach consensus when agreement cannot even be reached on basic definitions

The form and content of "bodies of knowledge" have received considerable attention over the years and project management is no exception. Chapter 7, describing the evolution in project management thinking, illustrates the resulting expansion of content.

It is not easy to reach a consensus, especially when there still exist different shades of opinion on the very terms "project" and "project management". Moreover, ideally some form of structure is needed but no one structure has yet become generally accepted.

Nevertheless, it is still possible to set down some ground rules for the inclusion or exclusion of particular knowledge and a workshop committee meeting in Denver as long ago as 1985 did this. This committee recognized that project management is complex, and if its body of knowledge is to be dealt with satisfactorily, then a framework is needed within which it is possible to organize and reference the various sub-topics. A summary of their findings follows.[1]

Objective

- To establish a systematic model/framework/structure for a project management body of knowledge (PMBoK)

Purpose

- To build on what is already known
- To organize and classify the overall scope
- To break up content into logical pieces, yet integrate the whole
- To store and retrieve knowledge
- To correlate and encourage consistency across educational programs

Characteristics

- Simple
- Logical
- Saleable
- Comprehensive
- Compatible
- Systematic
- Understandable

The committee members quickly recognized that a two-dimensional breakdown structure was too restrictive for adequately describing the interdependencies and interrelationships between the various project management functions. They also recognized the need to establish the scope and boundaries of a PMBoK that led to a number of conceptual models that are discussed in Chapter 6.

Ideally, the content of each project management function or knowledge area should increase in detail as you progress downwards. This results in a hierarchy as shown Figure A-3.[2]

M. H. Price suggested a set of criteria for the inclusion (or exclusion) of a function based on the assumption that there is a common set of characteristics.[3]

Level	Description	Content
0	Discipline	The complete project management system
1	Function	Scope, quality, time, cost, risk, etc.
2	Process	The specific series of activities or steps that lead to an output which is the title of the sub-process, e.g., budgeting, scheduling, organization, quality in design, etc. It is the "what" in "what is project management about?"
3	Activity or task	The work required to produce a specific output or deliverable. That is, the "how to get there"
4	Technique	Specific process tools available to aid or accomplish the activity

Figure A-3: Hierarchical structure of functional knowledge

Each characteristic defines a start-up task and results in information that can be consolidated to meet most of the requirements of the project management plan (or plans). These characteristics are summarized as follows:

Rules can be established for determining the different functional areas of project management

1. Every function is composed of one or more activities for which a specific organizational structure can be identified or developed

2. Every function has a specific set of deliverable products or services associated with it

3. Each set of deliverables or services has a corresponding set of work packages or tasks

4. Each set of work packages or tasks has a corresponding set of specifications or standards

5. A specific set of personnel skills are required to perform the work of each function

6. Responsibility for each work package or task in the function can be specifically assigned to an individual

7. Specific procedures can be identified or developed for management of the function and its component activities

8. Equipment, software, data or other resources needed to perform the function can be identified

9. Training needed to perform the function can be identified

10. Job descriptions can be developed for each person performing the work of the function

11. Specific criteria can be established to evaluate the performance of the work of the function

12. A set of management information system inputs and outputs can be identified for purposes of monitoring progress within the function

A.3   Hierarchy of project management learning & competence

Perhaps the first thing to recognize is that learning about project management is learning about a process, the process of managing change. Not just any sort of change, of course, because everyone recognizes that change is going on all the time, like clothes getting tighter, stairs getting steeper, and police officers getting younger, as every year goes by.

Book learning and successfully answering multiple-choice questions alone do not make anyone into a project manager. But it can enhance their personal performance

No, not that sort of change! We are speaking here of change that is carefully conceived, deliberately planned and expertly executed - all for someone's benefit. In short, the effective management of creative, constructive and beneficial change.

You should also clearly understand that "book learning" alone does not make anyone into a project manager or even a practitioner. Project management is both an art and science and, as such, does need documented knowledge, but it also needs practical experience and the development of intuitive ability.

So, you need to proceed up through a series of distinct levels. This progression is shown conceptually in Figure A-4.[4] The figure shows project management learning ranging from art to science, the corresponding content at each level, and how each level is best conveyed to students of the discipline for the betterment of project management practice.

Vehicles for learning

In general there are four distinct and progressive categories of instructional learning:

1. Lecture
2. Case study
3. Simulation, and

4. On-the-job training

These four levels roughly correspond to the first four levels shown in Figure A-4. However, it must also be noted that in project management the material studied should progress from the general to the specific.[5]

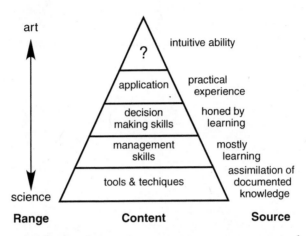

Figure A-4: Idealized progressive project management learning

The classroom lecture lends itself best to the study of project management tools, but is generally ineffective for the study of behavioral subjects, such as leadership, power, and politics. The problem with the latter is that real cases for study are generally out-of-date by the time they reach the classroom.

It is difficult to convey a feeling for real project management in a class room setting

Moreover, in a classroom it is difficult to construct an authentic situation that provides real experience of the application of the tools and techniques of the facilitating function subject areas except under very arbitrary circumstances. On the other hand, an actual case study on a real live project is necessarily project management application specific.

Simulation is a similar attempt to reproduce in the classroom the real socio-economic environment of project management and can embrace inter-organizational affairs, including owner-contractor relations and project performance. Computer programming can be used to control this learning environment.

"Role playing" is another form of classroom simulation that can be used to study and experience interpersonal relationships and small group dynamics. Both are important in the "matrix" organization environment as well as the single project.

The timing of on-the-job training relative to classroom learning is critical, but in the end essential

On-the-job training (OJT) is one of the most satisfactory and perhaps most common methods of instruction, i.e., learning by doing. It is obviously conducted by being involved in an actual project so is necessarily industry specific. Also, the quality of learning in this case is dependent upon the quality of the management of the particular project that may or may not be good. In other words, there is the possibility of bad habits being learned.

It has been suggested that it is possible to add only about 10% to an individual's knowledge base during each learning cycle, and that knowledge and experience must go together. Therefore, the timing of OJT in the individual's learning progress is quite critical. Too soon, and the student has no idea what can be learned and is of little use to the project. Too late, and the student is not only not equipped to take best advantage of class room learning, but may be difficult to teach.

However, timed correctly, OJT provides the student/practitioner the best learning combination. This way, students of project management can put into practice some of the tools and techniques learned in the classroom and conversely better understand classroom work experienced first hand.

References

[1] PMBOK 3/28/87, p0-3
[2] PMBOK 3/28/87, p4-2
[3] Price, M.H., PMI member. Abstracted from correspondence circa July 1990
[4] Ulmanis, V. Afterthoughts reported by I. Wirth from PMI/INTERNET Symposium, Atlanta, 1989
[5] Wirth, I. Abstracted from *Program Design in Project Management Education: A Road Map*, PMnetwork, May 1990, p39

Appendix B

Project management applications

B.1   Appropriate use of project management

Whether project management is appropriate for conducting a particular effort, and the degree to which project management should be applied, can be determined by answering the following questions:[1]

Fit

- Does it meet project definition by having defined objectives to be achieved that will signal completion?
- Is it unique, or at least relatively rare in some respect?
- Is it time and cost critical?
- Are resources limited in some way?

Challenge

- Is it large?
- Is it technically complex?
- Is the technology new?
- Might specific ad hoc opportunities or problems arise that must be dealt with?
- Do other concurrent projects exist that may have an impact on this one?
- Will it require quick response to changing conditions?
- Are results critical or especially important?

Organization

- Does it have strong top management support?

- Must it be coordinated across functional boundaries?
- Must resources be shared between organizational units or with other projects?
- Is it a case where organizational disruption must be minimized?
- Will multiple regulatory approvals require coordination?
- Will outside goods and services sources have to be managed?
- Will single point responsibility and reporting be an advantage or required?
- Will it require single point representation to the customer?

In the last analysis, whether or not a particular situation could or should be managed as a project requires a conscious decision one way or the other. The answers to the above questions should help you decide.

B.2 Range and diversity of projects

Examples of project management applications abound. Their range and diversity may be illustrated by the following (the lists are not intended to be exhaustive!):[2]

- Design, engineering, and construction of a highway, bridge, dam, canal, building, etc.
- Design and implementation of an urban (or rural) development program
- Restoration and upgrades, e.g., heritage buildings, buildings, infrastructure, services, equipment
- Design of a military project, e.g., submarine, fighter aircraft, tank, or military communications system
- Building a nuclear power plant
- Research and development of a new machine tool
- Development of a new product or manufacturing process
- Reorganizing a corporation
- Implementing a new administrative system
- Launching a marketing initiative

• Landing a man on the moon and returning safely to earth

The foregoing are perhaps the most obvious. Examples of even more common application include:

• Producing a stage play
• Writing a book
• Restoring an antique car
• Designing a new teaching course
• Building or remodeling a house
• Getting married (or divorced)

B.3   Typical list of industries using project management

• Aerospace
• Agriculture/Foods
• Amusements
• Automotive
• Banking
• Chemicals/Petroleum/Pharmaceuticals/Rubber and plastics/ Leather/ Metals
• Communications/Media
• Electronics/Instruments/Computers/Software
• Engineering/Design/Construction
• Finance/Insurance/Real estate
• Government and civil service
• Health care
• Hotels
• Lumber and wood products/Pulp and paper
• Mining
• Museums/Zoos
• Printing/Publishing
• Resource industries
• Services: Educational/Health/Legal/Social

- Ships/Boats/Marine
- Software/Hardware development
- Stone/Clay/Glass/Concrete
- Telecommunications
- Textiles
- Transportation/Railroads
- Utilities/Energy
- Volunteer Organizations
- Wholesale/Retail trade

B.4 Potential domains for project management[3]

A. *Grouped by broad functional similarity and suggested PMBoK affinity*

These domains cut across both manufacturing and services industries, are present in most organizations whether separate or combined, and can benefit from project management principles and practices.

• Architecture/Engineering/Design	Scope
• Construction	"
• Maintenance	"
• Manufacturing operations	"
• Research and development	"
• Environmental/Safety protection	Quality
• Quality assurance/Control/Inspection	"
• Corporate planning	Time
• Finance/Accounting	Cost
• Fund raising	"
• Insurance/Risk	Risk
• Personnel/People development/Training	H/R
• Purchasing/Procurement/Legal	C/P
• Communications/Public relations	Info/Comms

- Information systems/Records management   "
- Marketing/Sales   "

B.   *Grouped by broad product similarity*

Projects in these groupings of industry domains may be expected to have similar working environments.

- Aerospace
- Agriculture/Foods
- Air/Land/Sea Transportation
- Amusements/Museums/Zoos
- Chemicals/Pharmaceuticals/Petroleum/Plastics and rubber
- Commercial/Institutional/Residential construction
- Communications/Media
- Computers/Electronics/Instruments/Software
- Government/Defense
- Lumber/Wood/Pulp and paper products
- Manufacturing: AutomotiveConcrete/Clay/Glass/Leather/ Metals/Stone/Textiles
- Marine: Boats/Ships
- Political campaigning
- Printing/Publishing
- Private Services: Financial/Insurance/Legal/Real estate
- Public Services: Educational/Health/Social/Tourism
- Travel Accommodation
- Utilities
- Volunteer Organizations
- Wholesale/Retail trade

B.5   Potential advantages or benefits of project management

- Appropriate where effort qualifies as a project
- Goal focused, improved scope definition
- Results orientation, measurable output

- Increased visibility
- Greater quality conformance
- Reduced time
- Reduced cost
- Improved risk handling
- Single point of responsibility
- Better control (authority, responsibility, reliability and accountability)
- Greater team spirit
- Improved functional coordination and integration
- Increased individual morale
- Resource optimization
- Proactive management and improved effectiveness
- Greater consistency of approach and consequent efficiency
- Higher reliability
- Better customer relations
- Higher chances of success

B.6   Personal benefits

- Improved job satisfaction and greater personal involvement
- Excitement
- Challenge
- More motivation and commitment
- A feeling that you belong and are more valued
- Greater opportunity to gain experience and increase your contribution
- Enlarged personal skill sets and personal competitiveness
- Satisfaction of responsibility, authority, accountability, reliability
- Practice a more entrepreneurial and "bottom line" outlook
- Individuals become more valuable to the organization

- Hence, greater potential for promotion

B.7   Traps to avoid

- Inappropriate where effort does not qualify as a project
- Disorganization
- Disruptive conflict
- Special leadership skills missing
- Project management knowledge missing
- Trade-offs not understood
- Timely decisions missing
- Goodwill missing
- An appropriate cultural environment not established
- More difficult than traditional management
- Success not absolutely assured

B.8   When not to use project management[4]

- The business products or services are highly standardized
- The production processes are routine or seldom change
- The standard organizational framework is effective in making strategic and key operating decisions
- The technology is stable and well within the state-of-the-art
- The political, social, economic, technological and competitive environments are stable
- Projects are not an integral part of the organization's operations and do not require project management techniques
- The entity is small and the same results can be accomplished through the functional organization, even though "informal" project management techniques may be used

References

[1] After Stuckenbruck, L., *The Implementation of Project Management*, PMI 1981, p17-18

[2] After Cleland, D.I., *Project Management: Strategic Design and*

Implementation, Tab Books Inc., PA, 1990, p9

[3] Thatcher, J. R., in a letter to A. Stretton, Feb 8, 1990

[4] After Cleland, D.I., *Project Management: Strategic Design and Implementation*, Tab Books Inc., PA, 1990, p51

Appendix C

A short glossary
of project management terms

The following is a brief glossary of the most common project management terms and their most widely used meanings. Note that the project context is implicit throughout these definitions. For a comprehensive glossary, visit my web site.[1]

Accountability: Being answerable for results.

Amount at Stake: In the case of a risk event, the cost of adverse consequences that could occur to a project, including the cost of recovery. In the case of project shutdown, the value invested to date, including the cost of disposition.

Area of Project Application: The environment in which a project takes place, with its own particular culture, nomenclature and accepted practices.

Authority: One who is vested with power to give final endorsement, which requires no further approval.

Bar chart: A view of project data that uses horizontal bars on a time scale to show activity information. Frequently called a Gantt chart.

Baseline: A management plan and/or scope document fixed at a specific time in the project life span and used as a basis of reference.

Business Case: A document developed towards the end of the concept phase to establish the merits and desirability of the project, and justification for continuing into the following phase of project definition.

Change: The substitution of one thing in place of another.

Commitment: An agreement to consign or reserve the necessary resources to fulfill an obligation until the work or expenditure is completed. A commitment is an event.

Contract/Procurement Management: The function through which resources are acquired for the project in order to produce the end results. The practice of contract/procurement should include both internal (quasi-formal) commitments and external (formal-legal) contracts for people, services, materials and equipment.

Control: The planning, monitoring and analysis of accomplishment, and the exercise of any necessary corrective action to yield the required outcome.

Corporate Business Life Span: A life span which encompasses phases of policy planning and identification-of-needs that occur before a project is launched, as well as product-in-service and disposal after the project life span is completed. The management cycle of planning and budgeting is typically repeated on an annual basis.

Cost: The cash value of project activity.

Cost Management: The function required to maintain effective financial control of the project throughout its life span.

Critical Success Factors (CSF): Those measurable factors, listed in order of importance, that when present in the project's environment are most conducive to the achievement of a successful project. Examples include: Project objectives aligned with corporate mission; Top management support; A culture of open communication, etc. See also Key Success Indicators.

Customer: The immediate recipient of the product of the project, who will use it and is in the best position to evaluate its acceptability after a suitable period of learning.

Effort: The application of human and/or mechanical energy to accomplish an objective. See also Work.

Environment: The combined internal and external forces, both individual and collective that assist or inhibit the attainment of project objectives.

Executive Authority: The individual or collective body representing the source of project management's authority. This authority may be channeled through a project sponsor, or project director.

Executive Control Point: One or more points in the project life span at which the project's executive may exercise a go/no-go decision on the continuation of project activities.

Facilities/Product Life Span: A life span that encompasses the project life span as well as the phases of operation and disposal of the resulting product.

Feedback: Information (data) extracted from a process or situation and available to enable or assist positive control of that process. The data could indicate the need for re-planning or immediate modification of inputs (actions or decisions) into the process or situation.

Forecast: An estimate and prediction of future conditions and events based on information and knowledge available at the time of the forecast.

Function: (project management function.) The series of processes by which the project objectives in that particular area of project management (e.g. scope, quality, time, etc.) are achieved.

Human Resources Management: The function of directing and coordinating people throughout the life of the project by applying the art and science of behavioral and administrative knowledge to achieve the predetermined project objectives of scope, quality, time, cost, and customer satisfaction.

Information/Communications Management: The proper organization and direction of information, transmitted by whatever means, to satisfy the needs of the project.

Key Success Indicators (KSI): Those project management indicators that:
• are determined at the beginning of the project and listed in order of priority
• reflect directly on the key objectives of the project, and
• provide the basis for project management trade-off decisions during the course of the project
And, after completion of the project:
• are most likely to result in acceptance of the project and its product by the project's stakeholders as being successful in terms of customer satisfaction, and
• can be measured in some way, at some time, on some scale.
(See also Critical Success Factors.)

Management: The process of planning, organizing, executing, coordinating, monitoring, forecasting and exercising direction and control.

Monitoring: The capture, analysis and reporting of actual performance compared to planned performance.

Participant: See stakeholder.

Plan: An intended future course of action.

Portfolio Management: The management of a collection of relatively independent projects grouped into a "portfolio" to meet some business need such as overall management strategy, shared resources or funding, and/or relative risk assessment.

Process: The set of activities required to produce an output.

Professionalism: Being part of a body of people engaged in some practice in a superior way.

Program Management: The management of a series of related projects designed to accomplish broad goals to which the individual projects contribute, and typically executed over an extended period of time.

Project: A novel undertaking to create a new product or service the delivery of which signals completion. Projects are typically constrained by limited resources.

Project Brief: A major document typically prepared as the basis for an executive management go/no-go decision at an executive control point. Following a go decision, the document becomes the baseline or control basis for the project control cycle.

Project Charter: See project brief.

Project Control Cycle: The sequence of activities that are used to steer the project towards conformance with project requirements - see control.

Project Integration: The bringing together of diverse organizations, groups or parts to form a cohesive whole to successfully achieve project objectives.

Project Life Span: The four sequential phases that every project passes through, namely: concept; definition; execution; and transfer. These phases may be further broken down into stages that reflect the area of project application. These phases are also known by different names in different industries.

Project Management: The art of directing and coordinating human and material resources throughout the life of a project by using modern management techniques to achieve predetermined objectives of scope, quality, time, cost, and customer satisfaction. In short the art of getting things done effectively and efficiently.

Project Management Body of Knowledge (PMBoK): All subject areas covered in sufficient depth to understand and apply sound project management principles and practices necessary for the successful planning and accomplishment of projects. The generic PMBoK encompasses generally accepted "good project management".

Project Management Integration: The harmonizing of the four core project management functions of scope, quality, time and cost, through the four facilitating functions of risk, human resources, contract/procurement and information/communications. The objective is to satisfy the project's stakeholders and customers. Scope and quality reflect the technological requirements of the project.

Project Manager: The individual appointed with responsibility for project management of the project.

Project Organization: The orderly structuring of project participants.

Project Phase: The division of a project time frame (or project life span) into the largest logical collection of related activities.

Project Stage: A sub-set of project phase.

Project Success: A multi-dimensional construct that inevitably means different things to different people. It is best expressed at the beginning of a project in terms of key and measurable criteria upon which the relative success or failure of the project may be judged. For example, those that:
- Meet key objectives of the project such as the business objectives of the sponsoring organization, owner or user, and
- Elicit satisfaction with the project management process, i.e. that the deliverable is complete, up to standard, is on time and within budget, and
- Reflect general acceptance and satisfaction with the project's deliverable on the part of the project's customer and the majority of the project's community at some time in the future.

Project Team: The central management group headed by a project manager and responsible for the management and successful outcome of the project.

Public Relations: An activity designed to improve the environment in which an organization operates in order to improve the performance of that organization.

Quality Grade: The composite of all attributes or characteristics, including performance, of an item or product required to satisfy stated or implied needs. The use of the word "quality" on its own tends to imply the degree to which an item satisfies a particular quality grade, and not the grade itself as in the expression "poor quality". Quality grade is the most enduring in terms of project success.

Quality Assurance: The planned and systematic (managerial) actions necessary to provide adequate confidence that the item or product will satisfy given quality grade requirements.

Quality Control: The operational (technical) activities and techniques required to ensure conformance to requirements or that the quality grade requirements have been fulfilled.

Quality Management: The function required to determine and implement quality policy throughout the project life span. Quality management encompasses the sub-functions of establishing the quality grade, quality assurance and quality control to the required grade.

Responsibility: The duties, assignments, and accountability for results associated with a designated position in the organization.

Risk (Project Risk): The cumulative effect of the chances of certain occurrences that will adversely affect project objectives. It is the degree of exposure to negative events and their probable consequences. In project work, risk is the converse of opportunity.

Risk Management: The art and science of identifying, analyzing and responding to risk factors throughout the life of a project and in the best interests of its objectives. In project work, risk management encompasses both risk and opportunity.

S-Curve: A plot of cumulative progress against time that, in practice, typically follows the shape of the letter "S".

Schedule: A display of project time allocation. See Bar Chart

Scope (Product scope): The bounded set of verifiable end products, or outputs that the project team undertakes to provide to the project sponsor. The required set of end results or products with specified physical or functional characteristics.

Scope of Work: The work involved in the design, fabrication and assembly of the components of a project's deliverable into a working product.

Scope Management: The function of developing and maintaining project scope.

Sponsor: The generic name given to the source of the project manager's delegated authority. The sponsor may be owner, financier, client, project director etc. See Executive Authority.

Status: The condition of the project at a specified point in time.

Stakeholder: One who has a stake or interest in the outcome of the project.

System: A methodical assembly of actions or things forming a logical and connected scheme or unit.

Technique: Skilled means to an end.

Tetrad Trade-off: The graphical representation of the need to balance the objectives (or constraints) of scope, quality, time and cost.

Time: The measure of duration.

Time Management: The function required to maintain appropriate allocation of time to the overall conduct of the project through the successive phases of its life span.

Uncertainty: The possibility that events may occur which will impact the project either favorably or unfavorably. See also (project) Risk.

Well-managed Project: One that is optimized for effectiveness in its planning phases but emphasizes efficiency in its performing phases.

Work: The exertion of effort over a period of time.

Work Breakdown: A task-oriented "family tree" of activities that organizes, defines and graphically displays the total work to be accomplished in order to achieve the final objectives of the project.

Reference

[1] Wideman, R.M., *A Comparative Glossary of Project Management Terms* at http://www.maxwideman.com/pmglossary/index.htm

Index

ISBN 141202786-1

9 781412 027861